Marcel Proust

Titles in the series Critical Lives present the work of leading cultural figures of the modern period. Each book explores the life of the artist, writer, philosopher or architect in question and relates it to their major works.

In the same series

# Marcel Proust

Adam Watt

REAKTION BOOKS

*For Amy, Erin, Thomas, Cameron, Hamish and Henry,*
*whose lives are just beginning*

Published by Reaktion Books Ltd
33 Great Sutton Street
London EC1V ODX, UK

www.reaktionbooks.co.uk

First published 2013

Printed and bound in Great Britain
by Bell & Bain, Glasgow

British Library Cataloguing in Publication Data
Watt, Adam A. (Adam Andrew), 1979–
    Marcel Proust. – (Critical lives)
    1. Proust, Marcel, 1871-1922. 2. Novelists, French–20th
    century–Biography.
    I. Title II. Series
    843.9'12-dc23

ISBN 978 1 78023 094 8

# Contents

# Texts and Abbreviations

Quotations from Proust's novel are taken from the Vintage Classics edition of *In Search of Lost Time*, six volumes, translated by C. K. Scott Moncrieff (except for *Time Regained*, translated by Andreas Mayor and Terence Kilmartin), revised by Terence Kilmartin and D. J. Enright (London, 2000–2002). References are incorporated in the text using the volume title and page number (e.g. *Swann's Way*, 45), followed by Roman numeral volume number and page reference from the four-volume 'Pléiade' edition of *A la recherche du temps perdu*, edited by Jean-Yves Tadié et al. (Paris, 1987–9). Where my reading of the French is at odds with the Vintage translation I have modified this, indicated by 'trans. mod.'

Quotations from Proust's shorter writings are taken from *Against Sainte-Beuve and Other Essays*, translated by John Sturrock (Harmondsworth, 1988) and *Contre Sainte-Beuve précédé de pastiches et mélanges et suivi de essais et articles*, edited by Pierre Clarac and Yves Sandre (Paris, 1971); references take the abbreviated form *ASB* or *CSB*, each followed by page numbers. Sturrock's volume is a selection: where I cite only *CSB*, the material quoted has not been published in translation.

All references to Proust's correspondence (abbreviated to '*Corr.*', followed by a volume number and page reference) are to the *Correspondance de Marcel Proust*, ed. Philip Kolb, 21 vols (Paris, 1970–93). Translations from the correspondence, and from all other works in French, unless otherwise stated, are my own.

Marcel Proust photographed by Otto, 1896.

# Introduction

In 1908, during a period of intense creative exertion, a 37-year-old invalid, largely confined to his room, both parents dead, his appetite fluctuating, his dependence on caffeine and other stimulants shaping his peculiar, unsociable routine, sought to understand his constant application of pen to paper. 'Work:' he wrote, 'the search for what is profound in pleasure.'[1] Appearances and mythologies to the contrary, there *was* pleasure in this existence, and Marcel Proust (1871–1922) dedicated what remained of his life to this rewarding yet ruinous pursuit. Writing, at this early moment when the novel is taking shape in Proust's head and in his notebooks, is already described as a *recherche*, an active search that takes pleasure as its central focus. Not a dry, intellectual undertaking but an expansive exploration of the riches of our sensory engagement with our surroundings, our companions, the world at large. Sticking with the sensory imagery of which we find so much in Proust's writing, later on in his notes, out of which the shape of the mature novel emerges, he writes succinctly and beautifully of happiness that 'is but a certain sonority of the strings that vibrate at the slightest thing, and that a ray of sunshine can set singing'.[2]

The hope and the joy in this image sustained Proust through the years of composition of *A la recherche du temps perdu* (*In Search of Lost Time*) between 1908 and his death in 1922. He grappled for almost all of his adult life with the troubles of the introspective invalid, and the inevitable suspicions that the world beyond the isolation of his sickroom was one of great yet largely inaccessible delights. But Proust's life was not only one of seclusion, medication and self-pity. His creative life was dominated by solitude, starved of light and choked of air, but these hours spent propped up on pillows, pen in hand, were fuelled by an adolescence and early adulthood of travel, friendship and love and, in later years, time spent in Paris society of the belle époque, at lavish dinners, at the theatre and the opera. Thanks to the extraordinary transformative power of his mind he created a work of art that is populous, rich with character and social set-piece, bright with colour and alive with strings that vibrate, chords that make us sing. What sets *A la recherche* apart – besides its great and much maligned length – is the glue that holds this vast structure together, the first-person narrator whose unforgettable voice is that of an analytical poet-voyeur, an obsessive observer, theorizer and legislator. This narrator is shaped by Proust's experience, his passions and his losses, his fleeting joys, his self-scrutiny. But he is not Proust: he is a fictional creation.

Proust had an extraordinarily finely calibrated cultural compass, a mind always alert and delicately attuned to the artistic currents of his time, as well as to the earlier movements that had shaped the landscape which he surveyed. His childhood summers and his years as a student at the Lycée Condorcet in Paris provided the readerly nourishment that was stored up and drawn on in the later, sedentary years of creative seclusion. Contemporary innovations permitted ongoing connection to the outside world: telegrams and telephone calls (often sent or made by others on his behalf, under minutely detailed instruction) communicated his messages outwards; the Théâtrophone brought real-time performances from Paris's Opéra and theatres to his bedside. The young Proust was a thrilled passenger in a fast-moving automobile that tore through the Normandy countryside in the summer months, bringing into contact places hitherto thought wholly separate and isolated. Shortly after the turn of the century and before the devastation of losing his parents, Proust made travels further afield, an artistic tourist seeking illumination from Old Masters in Belgium and Holland. Venice was visited and its stones and waterways left their indelible mark in the author's memory. Later in life invitations to London would come, but were declined: the reader of George Eliot, of Hardy, Stevenson and Ruskin never set foot on British soil.

Popular perceptions of Proust frame him as a difficult author, an icon of high culture. He is encapsulated in a comfortable cliché: a mouthful of cake dipped in tea brings an unexpected flood of memory – the *madeleine* moment – yet relatively few read even as far as the pages where this experience is first described. Fewer still work through the volumes that follow and which, as we read on, over weeks and months, lead us, via echo, anticipation, repetition and replay, to gain our own sense of time regained. Proust's audacious experiment tells the life of an individual who wants to write a book but cannot, impeded by the unavoidable bumps in life's road: desire, vanity, jealousy, procrastination, illness, self-doubt. As we read on, looking over the shoulder of our guide, listening in on his thoughts, by turns rhapsodic and raging, we grow intimate with an extraordinary intellect, a sensitive witness to humankind and all its fragility. We live with Proust's narrator, absorbed in the world he inhabits. By the close of the novel, when, like Eliot's Prufrock, he sees 'the moment of [his] greatness flicker' and 'the eternal Footman hold [his] coat, and snicker', he is, of course, afraid, but he also is assured in the knowledge that the life he has lived will be the raw material for the book he must now write.

Proust's own life spanned times of radical social and cultural change. When so much about him (whether the measure is caffeine consumed, letters written or manuscript additions made) tends towards copiousness, writing a short book about Proust and his work is a challenging proposition. My debt to the authoritative biographies by Jean-Yves Tadié and William C. Carter is substantial and equalled only by that which I owe to the scholarship of Philip Kolb and Kazuyoshi Yoshikawa, respectively editor of Proust's 21-volume correspondence and director of its invaluable index. Drawing on these and many other sources, what follows seeks to tell the story of a highly idiosyncratic life and how it yielded one of the twentieth century's most important works of literary art. To consider critically Proust's life – his loves, doubts and suffering, his committed, profound, creative thinking – is to edge closer to understanding the foundations of the work he produced. It is hoped that the present volume might then move readers to turn their attentions, as Proust would have wished, (back) to that very work.

# 1

# Physician Heal thy Son

For everyone in Paris the twelve months between July 1870 and July 1871 were tumultuous, marked by upheaval and change. Napoleon III declared war on Prussia on 19 July 1870; by September that year he was captured at Sedan and his armies humbled; Paris was besieged for several months before yielding, then its citizens faced the humiliation of the victors parading through the streets. Although an armistice was signed on 28 January 1871, large numbers of Parisians were unwilling to accept defeat. They took control of the capital between March and May 1871 (the 'Paris Commune'), eventually being violently suppressed by forces loyal to the government in what is known as the '*semaine sanglante*' (bloody week) of 21–28 May 1871.

For Adrien Proust (1834–1903), an extremely talented and promising young doctor, the years preceding these momentous days had provided their own share of event and excitement. He left the village of Illiers in the Eure-et-Loir, about 25 kilometres from Chartres, to pursue his studies in Paris (he was the first of his family to do so) and in 1862 he received his medical degree. The following year he was named *chef de clinique* as a result of his performance in competitive state examinations; and in 1866 at the age of 32 he successfully defended his doctoral thesis on 'Different Types of Softening of the Brain' and passed the *concours d'agrégation*, a highly demanding public examination required by those wishing to teach, in this case in the Académie de Médecine. Beyond his academic study, his dedication and bravery in treating patients in Paris during the cholera epidemic of 1866 led the brilliant young physician to be invited by the French government to make a major voyage in 1869 to explore how previous outbreaks of the disease had spread, with a view to testing and developing means of containment using a cordon sanitaire. Over three months he travelled many thousands of kilometres, going from France to multiple sites in Germany and Russia, to Baku, Tehran and Istanbul, returning via Athens, Messina and Marseilles, tracing the paths taken by previous epidemics. His exhausting journey was made by train, by boat, by diligence (stagecoach) and by horse. Adrien Proust and Jules Verne (1828–1905), author of *Twenty-Thousand Leagues Under the Sea* and *Journey to the Centre of the Earth*, were contemporaries. Dr Proust's biographer likens his subject to 'Philéas Fogg, who toured the world, and with whom [Adrien] shares the same qualities of resilience and adaptability to his circumstances'.[1] The fruits of his exploration and enquiries on this extraordinary trip were condensed into a report published in the *Journal officiel* on 10–11 July 1870, which was well received by the ministers who had instigated the mission. Just over a week later, war was declared. Adrien's rise was unchecked by growing national turmoil, however, and on 8 August he was awarded the red ribbon of the Chevalier de la Légion d'Honneur for his services. Sometime, remarkably, during these hectic years Adrien made the acquaintance of Jeanne Weil (1849–1905). Jeanne was fifteen years Adrien's junior, an intelligent young woman who spoke and read English and German and played the piano, skills developed from her mother, Adèle Weil. While their courtship is largely a matter for speculation, it is known that Jeanne and Adrien signed a marriage contract on 27 August 1870 and were married in a civil ceremony on 3 September, the day after Napoleon III's capture at Sedan.

Subsequently, as Paris was besieged, as tensions rose, woodpiles dwindled, stores of flour grew bare and Parisians turned to the inhabitants of the city zoo for a source of meat, Dr and Madame Proust began their married life. Jeanne was soon pregnant and quickly grew anxious about bearing a child in such an unstable and often straightforwardly dangerous environment. Her husband shared her concerns but was not to be bowed by the barricaded streets and public disarray: his endeavours to date were testament to his great courage and devotion to his calling. His glittering career was very nearly cut brutally short, however: when his wife was six months pregnant, Adrien was shot at in the street on his way to the hospital. The bullet, fortunately, merely grazed his coat. In communard Paris, where the gunfire did not cease and hearses, ambulances and fleeing citizens, refugees from their own city, were everyday sights, Jeanne Proust, just seven months married, 'celebrated her twenty-second birthday in an apocalyptic atmosphere'.[2]

The Commune and its eventual bloody suppression took their course. After the *semaine sanglante*, when the journey was deemed to be safe, Jeanne was taken to the house of her uncle Louis Weil in Auteuil, to the west of the city. Here, as the dawn of the Third French Republic was breaking, in the comfort and safety of Louis' home, Jeanne gave birth on 10 July 1871 to a fragile, sickly baby boy: Marcel. Since returning from his mission to Russia and Persia, Adrien had become a Chevalier de la Légion d'Honneur and a husband; now, one year on, he was to begin a new mission as a father.

Adrien's was a Catholic, provincial family of modest means but long standing: Prousts can be traced back to the sixteenth century in the town of Illiers, where his parents had a grocer's shop. Jeanne's family was Jewish, originally from Württemberg in southern Germany but established for two generations in France, and extremely wealthy: her paternal grandfather had been a porcelain manufacturer in Paris and her father was a successful stockbroker. Although the lean and unstable times of the Commune had been hard, particularly for a young woman pregnant with her first child, the couple's life – and the life to which their offspring would become accustomed – was one of comfort and plenty. Although neither Adrien nor Jeanne practised their respective religion, they did follow social convention and had Marcel baptized. Normally this was done within three days of an infant's birth. The fragile state of the newborn's health was such, however, that he was not in fact baptized until 5 August. Gradually, though, he grew stronger and the family's worries subsided. When Marcel was 22 months old, Jeanne gave birth to another baby boy, Robert, again at Auteuil, on 24 May 1873. Her second son, also baptized in the Catholic faith, was much more robust than Marcel and caused his parents far less concern.

During this time the development of Adrien's career continued apace. As Mme Proust produced her second son her husband produced a book, which was the first of many. *An Essay on International Hygiene: Its Applications against Plague, Yellow Fever and Asiatic Cholera*, based on research from his trip of 1869, was well received by the medical community and was feted by the Institut de France. Soon the wish to be able to receive patients and colleagues at home, together with the needs of his newly expanded family, meant that Dr Proust needed to find new lodgings. From the apartment in the rue Roy into which he and Jeanne had moved as newlyweds, the family of four moved to a large apartment at 9 boulevard Malesherbes near the church of Sainte-Marie-Madeleine in the eighth arrondissement. This would be the family home for almost 30 years.

Dr Proust's professional reputation as an authority in the new and burgeoning field of hygiene was growing. When he was not at clinics in the Paris hospitals in which he served or at the Institution Sainte-Perrine in Auteuil, reports and articles, often based upon first-hand clinical observation, flowed steadily from the desk in his gloomy office in the apartment on boulevard Malesherbes: as

Dr Adrien Proust, engraving after a drawing by Henri Meyer, 1884.

many as sixteen in the period between the publication of the *Essay on International Hygiene* in 1873 and his *Treatise on Public and Private Hygiene* of 1877. The latter, weighty volume (more than 800 pages long), which would become a standard work in the field, was augmented in the second edition of 1881 and expanded further in a third edition, prepared with the aid of two colleagues, in 1882–3. During this same period Adrien travelled a good deal, representing France at international congresses in Vienna, Brussels, Turin and Geneva, insistently arguing the case for the adoption of sanitary controls by the international community. In 1879 his standing and reputation were cemented with his election to membership of the Académie de Médecine.

Given his father's volume of work and travel, it is unsurprising, perhaps, that from early childhood Marcel developed a much stronger bond with his mother. This would remain a defining aspect of his character throughout his life. As Marcel and Robert grew up, they were cared for at home in Paris by their mother and their maternal grandmother. Easter holidays were spent in Illiers with the Proust side of the family at the home of Adrien's sister Elisabeth and her husband Jules Amiot; shorter breaks during the year and the summer holidays were spent in Auteuil, at the house where the boys were born and to which, in a gesture of characteristic generosity, Louis Weil added a wing in 1876 for the family to use as their own. Louis cared greatly for his family but his generosity also served a personal need for privacy: having amassed a significant fortune as a manufacturer of buttons and through his marriage to the daughter of a wealthy banker, as a widower in the 1870s he was childless and wealthy, a bon viveur with a passion for beautiful actresses and singers, whose photographs he collected as mementos of his affairs. His lovers included the famous *demi-mondaine* Laure Hayman, an alluring, intelligent and headstrong individual who inspired, among others, the creative energies of the painter James Tissot and the writer Paul Bourget, for whom she served as the model for the protagonist in his novella *Gladys Harvey* (1888). In Proust's novel, Louis' traits can be found in the fictional Uncle Adolphe, by whose exotic and alluring companion, 'the lady in pink', the young narrator is entirely bewitched. The lady in pink – at the time of her appearance under that name she is Adolphe's lover, but will later become Mme Swann, the woman who is said by the bourgeois of Combray to be '*une femme de la pire société, presqu'une cocotte*' (a woman of the worst type, almost a prostitute; *Swann's Way*, 22; 1, 20) – has many of the traits of Laure Hayman. In 1888, after meeting the adolescent Marcel and receiving numerous bouquets of flowers from him, Hayman made him what would become a treasured gift: a copy of Bourget's tale, bound in the silk of one of her petticoats.

Before this moment, one of a number of part-initiations into the world of adult passions, Marcel's early years were largely

unremarkable: happy and relatively active. At Auteuil and at Illiers
there were large gardens to explore and in which to play. At Illiers
the surrounding countryside provided terrain for adventures, long
walks along the banks of the Loir, fishing and contemplation of the
unfolding beauty of the landscape through the seasons. Ever mindful
of her boys' intellectual development, even during the holidays
Jeanne saw that Marcel and Robert had piano lessons; and they
learned their Latin and German verbs amid hunts for flowers and
plants they could identify in the fields. Marcel's precocious learning
is attested in a letter that has survived from February 1881, written
in German to his maternal grandmother, alluding to his ongoing
Latin learning, fully nine months before he started at the *lycée*. As
a young boy in Illiers Proust's preferred occupations were reading
– a habit developed and encouraged by his mother and above all
his maternal grandmother – and observing the delights of nature,
so different to the sights and sounds offered to his senses in
Haussmann's Paris. In an essay written in 1905 as a preface for
his translation of John Ruskin's *Sesame and Lilies*, Proust wrote
memorably about the bliss of childhood reading:

> There are no days of my childhood which I lived so fully perhaps
> as those I thought I had left behind without even living them,
> those I spent with a favourite book. Everything which, it seemed,
> filled them for others, but which I pushed aside as a vulgar
> impediment to a heavenly pleasure: the game for which a friend
> came to fetch me at the most interesting passage, the trouble-
> some bee or shaft of sunlight which forced me to look up from
> the page or to change my position, the provisions for tea which
> I had been made to bring and which I had left beside me on the
> seat, untouched, while, above my head, the sun was declining
> in strength in the blue sky, the dinner for which I had had
> to return home and during which my one thought was to
> go upstairs straight away afterwards, and finish the rest of the

Proust as a child, photographed by Félix 'Nadar', date unknown.

chapter: reading should have prevented me from seeing all this as anything except importunity, but, on the contrary, so sweet is the memory it engraved in me (and so much more precious in my present estimation than what I then read so lovingly) that if still, today, I chance to leaf through these books from the past, it is simply as the only calendars I have preserved of those bygone days, and in the hope of finding reflected in their pages the houses and the ponds which no longer exist.[3]

The lines quoted here give a taste of how far the adult Proust recognized the value of this particular childhood pleasure, one which we can seldom, if ever, recapture as adults with greater worldly cares than the children and adolescents we once were. The closing lines in part prefigure how the narrator in *A la recherche* views his relation to his past in Combray when he looks back as an adult.

Molière and Racine, among others, had summer residences in Auteuil during the reign of Louis XIV, and in the nineteenth century Victor Hugo and the Goncourt brothers found peace and quiet there. It was also the site of the family home of Jacques-Emile Blanche, the renowned *fin-de-siècle* painter; here, in 1893, Blanche painted Proust's portrait in oils. In a preface Proust wrote in 1918 to a book of essays by the painter, he reflected revealingly on his memories of Auteuil:

I cannot say what pleasure I felt when, after coming along the rue La Fontaine in full sunlight, amid the scent of the lime trees, I went up for a moment into my bedroom where the unctuous air of a warm morning had finished glazing and isolating the simple smells of the soap and of the mirror-wardrobe, in a chiaroscuro made nacreous by the reflection and sheen of the tall Empire-blue satin curtains (not very rural); when, after stumbling across the small drawing-room, hermetically sealed against the heat, where a single shaft of daylight, seductive and unmoving, had finished anaesthetizing the air, and the pantry where the cider – that would be poured out into glasses which were a little too thick, so that you felt like biting into them as you drank, like some women's flesh, coarse in texture, when you kiss them – had grown so cold that when, in a little while, it was introduced into your throat, the weight of it would adhere totally, delectably, profoundly to the sides – I finally entered the dining room, its atmosphere congealed and transparent like some immaterial agate veined by the aroma of the cherries already piled in the fruit-dishes, and where, following the most vulgarly bourgeois custom, yet which enchanted me, the knives were propped on little glass prisms. The iridescence of these last did not merely add a certain mystical quality to the smell of the Gruyère and the apricots. In the penumbra of the dining room, the rainbow of these knife-rests cast peacock-eyes on to the walls that to me seemed as wonderful as the stained-glass windows – preserved only in the exquisite plans and transpositions that Helleu has given us of them – of Rheims cathedral, that cathedral which barbarous Germans so loved that, unable to take it by force, they threw vitriol at it. ('Preface' in *ASB*, 245–60 [247–8]; *CSB*, 570–86 [573])

This description of a most ordinary experience – moving from the outside world to an indoor setting – is sinuous, richly sensual and multifaceted, like the rainbow colours diffracted across the dining-room wall by the knife-rests of which the mature Proust is so critical. Both form and content here are redolent of the narrator's account of the house at Combray in *A la recherche*: the detail in the observations and the constantly transformative accounts of the sensory stimuli that are met (air that 'glazes' smells, light that 'anaesthetizes' air, a mineral-like atmosphere 'veined' by scents) are communicated by sentence structures whose complexity identifies them as those of an older individual looking back rather than the candid observations of the youthful individual whose experiences are described. The sense in this passage of a lost past accessible only through memories chimes with that quoted above from 'Days of Reading'; together they give us a sense of the continuity of Proust's writing and the extensive degree to which his past served as raw material for his literary endeavours.

Beyond the sights and smells of Auteuil and Illiers, many of the people whom Proust interacted with in those privileged places of his childhood lent shape and substance to the fictional figures who came to populate the world of his novel. To take just one example, Elisabeth and Jules Amiot had a maid named Ernestine Gallou, who was in their service in Illiers for over 30 years. This formidable woman appears under her own name in the notes Proust wrote for the novel he never completed, posthumously entitled *Jean Santeuil*. She provided memorable meals and household comforts to the visiting Prousts at Illiers and in many ways she can be seen and heard in the figure of Françoise in *A la recherche*, whom we first encounter, as the young narrator describes her in Combray, 'motionless and erect, framed in the small doorway of the corridor like the statue of a saint in its niche' (*Swann's Way*, 61; I, 52).

At Illiers bedtimes were enlivened for the boys by magic lantern shows: a projector was fitted on top of an oil lamp and manipulated so that coloured slides depicting tales such as that of Geneviève de Brabant were projected on to the walls of the room for the bewitched audience. Proust's maternal grandmother encouraged Marcel to read the novels of George Sand as a young boy; with the magic lantern we find another initiation into storytelling of a different sort. The colourful slides have a captivating transformative power: the projected images from the lantern changed the banal surface of the bedroom curtains, walls and doorway into a whole new realm of possibility and intrigue. These moments are recalled in the notes for *Jean Santeuil* and in the childhood scenes in 'Combray'. As the narrator bears witness to the unfolding story of the beautiful Geneviève and the wicked Golo, the lantern 'substituted for the opaqueness of my walls an impalpable iridescence, supernatural phenomena of many colours, in which legends were depicted as on a shifting and transitory window' (*Swann's Way*, 8; I, 9).

The more we discover of Illiers and Auteuil, the more we realize that Proust's fictional Combray is a composite, a place whose hills and plains, streams, fields, place names, even its weather, are woven from countless strands of remembered, adapted and imagined experience. Méréglise, Tansonville, Montjouvin, Martinville, Vieuvicq: near Illiers one finds place names that now echo, now overlap with those we find in the imaginary topography of *A la recherche*. Near Illiers run the waters of the Thironne and the Vilaine, rivers whose names together seem to whisper 'Vivonne', the fictional river that wends through Combray. While the surroundings in which Proust grew up undoubtedly contributed to the picture that is developed in 'Combray', there is one glaring difference between the real and fictional worlds: the narrator who inhabits the pages of *A la recherche* is without siblings.

When asked to recall his earliest childhood memories, Robert Proust remarked that what always came to mind was the time around 1876, when Marcel was five and he was three: he remembered his brother looking out for him with 'infinite, enveloping sweetness', a quality of affection that he defined, intriguingly, as 'maternal'.[4] And this image, he states, is always associated with that of *la campagne ensoleillée* (the sunny countryside). Marcel and Robert were city dwellers for most of their lives, but there was no doubt that childhood happiness was inextricably associated with the pleasures of nature and the outdoor life. Although no brother for the narrator is written into Proust's novel, there is an intriguing scene contained in Proust's draft material that gives a snapshot of their childhood together and shows how his early family life became transmuted into the novel's final form.

In the opening volume of Proust's novel we encounter a scene in which the child narrator is found by his mother on the little path near the house at Combray, trying to take his beloved hawthorn bushes into his arms, distraught that he must leave them – and the bewitching profusion of perfume and colour that their blossoms offer – behind on his imminent, parentally imposed departure for Paris. Such a scene, it seems, was a reality on one family holiday, probably in 1878, but with Robert as the protagonist and, curiously, a goat rather than hawthorn bushes as the object of his affections. Both boys were angry with their mother, who had not forewarned them that she would be leaving to visit a friend and taking Robert with her. These actions were doubly cruel in the boys' minds: they would separate Marcel from his mother, the person he loved most in the world (a separation he could scarcely bear), and they would cut short Robert's enjoyment of the company of the animal with whom he had developed a strong bond on this particular country

Proust and his brother Robert in Scottish dress, 1877.

retreat. On the same day, another member of the family had taken Robert to be photographed (this detail makes its way into the novel too, where it is the narrator who is to be photographed). As was bourgeois habit at the time, the young boy was dressed up in finery suitable for the occasion: Robert's hair was curled and adorned with ribbons and he wore a dress with a lacy skirt and matching satin accessories. When it was time for Mme Proust to leave for her visit, Robert, even so attired, was nowhere to be found. Finally Marcel and his mother found him on a distant path, cutting a rather pathetic figure with his beloved goat, his eyes red with tears and his finery in disarray, wailing 'My poor little goat, it wasn't you who wanted to make me unhappy, to separate me from those I love . . . You aren't nasty, not like them.'[5] Eventually the little boy agreed to go to the station with his mother but only on the condition that the goat is brought along too.

When they reached the station, Robert made one final statement of his case, handing the goat's tether to Marcel and throwing himself on the railway tracks, refusing to yield until he got his way. 'Fortunately', writes Proust in his sketch of this event, 'my father appeared at this moment.' Robert was prised from the tracks and the goat returned to the local farmer. Marcel's brother, smarting from the blows delivered by Dr Proust and 'staring fixedly' at his father 'with a concentrated fury, cried "I won't lend you my handcart ever again!"' Robert's suggestion that he had been made to suffer so much that he would deny his father his prized handcart contributes bathos to the scene, reminding us of how uncomprehending children can be of adult logic and decision-making. Seeking to smooth things over before leaving with her bedraggled younger son, Proust's mother told Marcel: 'You are older: be reasonable, please, and don't have a sad look when I leave: your father is already aggrieved that I am leaving – try not to have him find both of us unbearable.' These lines sympathetically frame the mother's perennial dilemma of keeping her husband happy and her progeny in line.

In the novel, the scene is recast with the narrator centre stage, rather than in the role of observing elder sibling. Robert's distress and sense of injustice clearly struck a chord with Marcel, for much of the wording of the scene of the narrator's farewell to the hawthorns draws directly on the sketch of Proust's younger brother. "'Oh my poor little hawthorns,'" we read the narrator wailing through his sobs in 'Combray', "'it isn't you who want to make me unhappy, to force me to leave you. You, you've never done me any harm. So I shall always love you'" (*Swann's Way*, 173–4; I, 143). The hawthorns for the narrator of the novel are an introduction to the beauty of nature and how hard it is for us to articulate the sense of awe it is capable of provoking; they confront the narrator with an almost overpowering sensual experience; and, in part, they point the way to a budding, youthful awareness of eroticism (the pink blossoms embedded in the hedge of white flowers are 'as different . . . as a young girl in festal attire among a crowd of dowdy women in everyday clothes'; *Swann's Way*, 168; I, 138). One can hardly imagine a goat performing this multiplicity of roles. Moreover, in the novel the wonders of nature embodied in the hawthorn bushes provide an unforgettable frame for the narrator's first glimpse of Gilberte Swann, his first childhood crush and one of the enduring loves of his life.

Marcel's unchecked enjoyment of the outdoors, however, was short-lived. When he was eight years old he tripped and fell while playing in the Champs-Elysées, breaking his nose. While this was hardly a life-threatening injury, it is quite possible that it played its part in the momentous shift in his health – and his mode of existence – that occurred the following year, in the spring of 1881. The family had been for a walk in the Bois de Boulogne with friends when, on their return home, Marcel suddenly began to struggle for breath and collapsed. This first asthma attack was so severe that he very nearly died in his father's arms. Robert recalled the event years later, remarking that the choking fit terrified his father and marked a dark new beginning for Marcel: 'from that day dates this dreadful life above which constantly hovered the threat of similar attacks.' Marcel, whose early years had been so enchanted and enlivened by the sights and smells of the shifting seasons in the countryside and in the new open spaces of Haussmann's Paris, was now forced to accept a renunciation of 'all that was the joy of the outdoors, the beauty of the countryside, the charm of flowers' for fear of triggering further, potentially fatal reactions.[6]

Proust's asthma, the development of his hay fever and severe sensitivity to dust, pollen and scents, teamed with his own severe anxieties about the potential repercussions of exposure to such, quickly led him into a spiral of strictures and seclusion. After his years of freedom, sensory stimulation and the joys these had brought, Proust must have felt that a whole world of experience was now lost to him. In the year before his death he recalled these early years of his illness in a letter, explaining that he was told that nasal cauterizations would destroy the erectile tissue in the nose and prevent the irritant action of pollen: 'I had such faith that I underwent 110 cauterizations, which were no fun at all.' He was then encouraged to go out into the countryside where, he was told, he would discover that further suffering had been rendered impossible. 'I left with my parents. At the first lilac in bloom that I would have sworn to be innocuous, I was seized by such asthma attacks that even once they got me back to Paris I had the purple feet and hands of the drowned' (*Corr.*, xx, 403). In a novella written probably in 1893–4, much nearer the time of the shock of his initial attack, Proust wrote movingly about the asthmatic's fearsome, despairing fight 'for the lost tranquillity that he will find again only with air from which he did not realize it to be inseparable'.[7] The experience of fighting for breath, the fear it instils in the sufferer and the desire it provokes for what seems lost, were of foundational importance to the young Marcel: as William Carter has noted, the original French of the line just quoted contains the verbs *perdre* and *retrouver* ('*sa tranquilité perdue qu'il ne retrouvera . . .'*), which would become central to the novel to which he would devote such a major part of his life.[8]

The etiology of Proust's asthma is a subject of some debate. That it contributed to or perhaps stoked the numerous neuroses and psychopathologies he developed in the course of his adult life (his fears of draughts, of dust, of chills, his concerns about cleanliness) is in little doubt. Some critics and biographers, most influentially among them Proust's first English-language biographer, George Painter, have argued that Proust, desperately jealous and fearful of having to compete for his mother's affections with his younger brother, somehow *chose* his asthma in order to gain the upper hand from Robert and secure his mother's undivided attention. On this reading Proust's ailments were at root psychosomatic afflictions, willed into being by the boy's nervous anxieties. There is no conclusive evidence, however, of this jealousy; moreover we now have a better understanding of asthma and we know that genetic and environmental factors are contributing causes.

Although we do not know for certain how Proust's asthma and allergies originated, we do know that he was a sickly baby and a weak infant. In the notes for *Jean Santeuil* and in *Swann's Way* we encounter a striking childhood scene that centres on a very needy, demanding child, who cannot bear to go to bed without the succour of his mother's kiss and who dissolves hopelessly into nervous crisis should the kiss be (or threaten to be) withheld. When his parents have an evening guest and the mother is unable to tuck in and kiss the young boy goodnight (Jean is described as seven years old, the narrator in 'Combray' is of indeterminate age), he takes matters into his own hands, accosting his mother tearfully when she does finally come upstairs, prompting his father unexpectedly to agree to the mother spending the night in the boy's room. The parents' concession is double-edged, for the boy is granted what he most wants, yet his enjoyment of his mother's presence is marred by the understanding that it will never be repeated. There is no concrete evidence from Proust's correspondence or elsewhere to confirm that such scenes took place between Marcel and Mme Proust. Nevertheless, the picture of intimacy, tenderness, anxiety and dependence that emerges from their later correspondence is wholly consonant with the troubling relationship to which we are privy in the 'bedtime drama' scenes of *Jean Santeuil* and 'Combray'.

Some of the suffering to which Proust attests in his correspondence, particularly with his mother, later in life (and there is scarcely a single letter in which some ailment, ache or anxiety is not described or dissected) was doubtless exaggerated or used as a lever or expedient. But it is important not to be overly hasty in pigeonholing Proust as another *malade imaginaire*, a whinging hypochondriac with little more wrong with him than idleness. He *was* a lifelong invalid, suffering more or less acutely from ailments ranging from arthritis, bronchial asthma and hay fever to insomnia, otitis media, pneumonia and uraemia.[9] The study of nervous illness during Proust's youth was a growing field of medical-scientific research; in a major work, *American Nervousness: Its Causes and Consequences*, published in 1881, the year Marcel succumbed to his first asthma attack, the American neurologist George Beard laid out his vision of a nation increasingly yielding, as a result of the ever-intensifying pace and pressure of modern life, to all manner of nervous ailments. Neurasthenia (or nervous exhaustion) was the cover-all term for a condition that manifested itself through a variety of symptoms and maladies presenting individually or in combination, such as anxiety, depression, headaches, fatigue and neuralgia. Proust would suffer from all of these complaints throughout his lifetime as well as, of course, from asthma, which in the late nineteenth century was considered to be a nervous illness. There is something of a painful irony in the fact that the celebrated Dr Proust, in collaboration with his colleague Gilbert Ballet, made a substantial contribution to the European understanding of nervous illness in 1897 with the work *L'Hygiène du neurasthénique* (*Treatment of*

*Neurasthenia*). The broader reach of this work (it was widely read in France and was published in English translation in 1902) was sadly not mirrored closer to home: Marcel was in boyhood, and remained throughout his adult life, someone for whom untroubled health was very seldom a reality.

André Maurois, in one of the earliest biographical studies of Proust, wrote that Marcel was a 'mixed strain' of his parents' characteristics: 'the contribution made by Dr Adrien Proust was a high seriousness, a scientific approach to life which Marcel was to inherit. To this his mother added a love of letters and a delicious sense of humour.'[10] Indeed he inherited, by and by, his father's scientific rigour and curiosity and this, coupled with the bookishness developed on his mother's side, meant that as he grew up he read and digested his father's own writings and gradually absorbed an ample knowledge of sickness and medicine that would colour his outlook on the world and inform the novel he came to write.

In suffering a major asthmatic seizure in 1881 Proust received intimations of mortality of the kind most of us are spared until much later in life. Additionally, key in his trajectory as an individual with artistic, creative leanings is the fact that this change in his bodily well-being served cruelly to place a virtual embargo on a whole gamut of experience and activity that he had already savoured with great relish. The sudden, forced moment of maturation that this most likely precipitated should not be underestimated. It surely shifted his outlook significantly: life presents abundant pleasures and satisfaction, but from this point onward such pleasures may only be experienced in memory; they cannot be seized for fear of the harm they might cause. Yet if such pleasures cannot be seized, perhaps they can be recalled, imagined and replayed, just like the tales of Geneviève de Brabant that flickered across the bedroom wall at Illiers.

## 2

# Asthmatic Absentee /
# Marcel *Militaire*

In our lives the days are not all equal. To get through each day, natures
that are at all highly strung, as was mine, are equipped, like motor
cars, with different gears. There are mountainous, arduous days, up
which one takes an infinite time to climb, and downward-sloping days
which one can descend at full tilt, singing as one goes.

*Swann's Way*

These lines serve us well if we seek an account of the character of
Proust's life in the years immediately following the experience
of his first asthma attack in the Bois de Boulogne. Proust's years
of senior school, beginning in 1882 at the Lycée Condorcet, a
well-to-do school in the ninth arrondissement, were full of ups
and downs. There were a great many mountainous days when
Marcel's health simply did not allow him to make it into school
at all; he began his fourth year at the *lycée* in October 1885 but his
health was so poor that his parents formally withdrew him at the
end of December that year. He would spend the following months
mainly at home, working on his French composition, among other
things, with private lessons bolstering his mother's earnest super-
vision. Life, though, was not all wheezing and confinement to the
sickroom: his health did improve and he began his fourth year
afresh in October 1886. Marcel's years as a *lycéen* were, health
problems aside, predominantly happy ones, marked by a good
number of downward-sloping days, many of them enjoyed if not

in full-voiced song, then certainly reciting poetry and playing games in the gardens of the Champs-Elysées. As his eldest son moved haltingly through the *lycée* classes, Adrien's career moved ever more smoothly through the gears. He published twelve articles and a second book, *Cholera: Etiology and Prophylaxy*, in 1883; twenty articles in 1884; and in October 1885 Adrien became Professor Proust, elected to the Chair of Hygiene at the Faculty of Medicine. After the enforced absence from his school companions from January to October 1886, Marcel began, perhaps against expectation, to move through the gears himself. Vast quantities of reading matter were consumed, within and often well beyond the school curriculum. He showed interest and ability in natural sciences and considerable aptitude in French and in history; prizes, mostly honourable mentions, were won, friends and progress – academic, intellectual, spiritual – were made. After four introductory years of broad-based and wide-ranging schooling, *lycée* students rounded off their education with the *classe de rhétorique* (or lower sixth-form), and the final year, the *classe de philosophie*.[1] This latter was greatly anticipated by Proust and, unlike so many experiences to which we look forward, weaving around them hopeful narratives of satisfaction and achievement, it did not disappoint. Turning eighteen in June and achieving his *baccalauréat* in August 1889, just a few months after the grand inauguration of Eiffel's tower, the entrance arch to the Exposition Universelle (World's Fair), Marcel was now a man with important choices to make about his future in a city that, for many of the 39 million people who visited the Exposition, seemed to be the capital of the modern world. Perhaps surprisingly, given his health record, upon finishing his time at Condorcet Marcel signed up for a year's military service. He lived the life of a cadet from 1889–90 and experienced for the first time real separation from his mother. He also tasted the pangs of bereavement when his adored grandmother Adèle Weil died in January 1890. These were the mountain climbs and exhilarating descents of his passage from boyhood to manhood. But, as we shall see, although the boy became a man, in many ways he remained his mother's *petit Marcel*.

While the site of the Lycée Condorcet was originally a Capuchin monastery, its appeal for many was that of an institution lacking the monastic severity of the prestigious schools on the Left Bank – Henri-iv, Louis-le-Grand and Saint-Louis – which were renowned for their relentless work ethic and success at preparing pupils for the gruelling entrance examinations for France's *grandes écoles*, the elite establishments of higher education that produce so many of the country's politicians, civil servants and leaders. Condorcet had a solid reputation and some illustrious alumni, an awareness of whom spurred intellectual ambition in the pupils of the school: the Goncourt brothers, the great chroniclers of nineteenth-century life, studied there, as did the poets Théodore de Banville and Paul Verlaine; Sainte-Beuve, the critic whose views Proust would take to task some years later; the historian and critic Hippolyte Taine; and the philosopher Henri Bergson (to whose ideas Proust's are often compared). Although there was an emphasis on literary study (and philosophy as we shall see), the school also counted among its alumni three statesmen who held office as President of the Republic during Proust's lifetime: Sadi Carnot (assassinated by an anarchist in office in 1894), Jean Casimir-Perier and Paul Deschanel.

Like many children of bourgeois families living in the eighth arrondissement, throughout his school years Marcel spent a lot of time playing in the Parc Monceau and, above all, in the gardens of the Champs-Elysées, where he would go after school with his classmates. When he was unable to go to class he was in fact encouraged to take the air, despite his respiratory problems, and would go to the gardens where he met with a number of young girls, some of whom remained companions for much of his life. Highly sensitive to the cold, he would go in the winter months with hot potatoes or grilled chestnuts in his pockets to keep his hands warm. Marcel enjoyed the company of Antoinette and Lucie Faure, whose parents were friends of the Proust family. Antoinette was the same age as Marcel and Lucie was five years older; their father, Félix Faure, succeeded Casimir-Perier as President of the Republic in 1895 and died four years later, in flagrante with his mistress. Marcel also played with two pretty young girls of noble Russian-Polish descent, Marie and Nelly de Bénardaky; much later in life he would describe Marie as 'the great love of [his] youth' as well as the 'intoxication and despair of my childhood' (*Corr.*, XVI, 163; XVII, 175). Marie is thought to be Proust's main inspiration for the young girl called Marie Kossichef in the notes for *Jean Santeuil*; it is likely that his interaction with all of these girls, and others, such as Jeanne Pouquet, informed the depiction of the narrator's relationship with Gilberte Swann in the mature novel.

The Champs-Elysées, as well as being a place to play games and to talk with other children, had the advantage of being somewhere he could indulge his passion for observation: he could contemplate nature and watch the elegant ladies as they strolled, absorbing details of form, dress and comportment. Marcel, not keen on the more energetic games in which his companions engaged, liked instead to speak to their mothers; his manners, intelligence and eloquence made a striking impression. Robert Dreyfus, one of Proust's schoolmates, wrote later that the gardens were 'in some ways the first "salon" in which the luminous gifts of his magnificent artistic intelligence and his delicious sensibility were to shine. An exceptional person, a child of original and vertiginous precocity, he charmed his little friends who were often much more coarse, and he stunned them somewhat.'[2] And so the young Proust, around the time he finished at Condorcet, graduated almost seamlessly from the outdoor, childhood delights of the Champs-Elysées to the indoor, adult spaces of the salons where the aspiring and wealthy bourgeois of Paris were received alongside the artists of the day by hostesses who, in some cases, were the mothers of his schoolmates.

Proust seems always to have been fascinated by older women. In a letter sent to his grandmother as a fourteen- or fifteen-year-old, he gives a thumbnail portrait of Mme Catusse, a fellow guest he and his mother met on a trip to the thermal spa resort of Salies-de-Béarn. Marcel writes:

> Mme Catusse must be twenty-two to twenty-five years old. A delightful head, two sweet and clear eyes, fine and white skin, a head worthy of being dreamed by a painter enamoured with perfect beauty, framed in pretty black hair. (Oh! The unbearable task of braving Musset and saying, above all when one thinks it, Madame, you are pretty, extremely pretty. But the divine melodies of Massenet and Gounod will calm my troubles). (*Corr.*, I, 95)

The teenager's estimate of age is a little off (Mme Catusse was 27 or 28 at this time) but his description shows an eye for detail and an aptitude for portraiture; the allusions to Musset and the music of Massenet and Gounod (famed above all for their works inspired by Goethe) show the teenager's absorption of the artistic production of the Romantic period.

The young Proust, then, exhibited an observant and socially inquisitive eye, coupled with a precocious and burgeoning enthusiasm for the arts. Childish traits remained, however, as another letter from Salies-de-Béarn testifies. The fifteen-year-old Proust recognizes a split in his feelings with which he struggles to come to terms: he is sad that his grandmother is not with him yet concurrently happy with the material circumstances of his vacation, a combination of emotions that results in his being 'prey to a very complex feeling which I'm a little ashamed to analyse'.

Having announced this conflicted state, Marcel launches into his reasons for happiness: 'This morning (I take a day at random and I consumed less today than usual) I ate: a boiled egg, two slices of steak, five whole potatoes, a cold chicken drumstick, a cold chicken thigh, three helpings of baked apples.' This list is followed by a request that its recipient keep it confidential since it suggests that 'an insatiable eater' has taken the place of 'the delicate scholar' ('*le lettré délicat*'). He fears creating the impression that the 'peaceful reader of Horace and Virgil' has been transformed into an 'enormous Pantagruel' (*Corr.*, XXI, 543). Here we find an interesting snapshot of the teenage Proust's book-ish self-image, and witness his pleasure, coloured by bashfulness, at his new-found appetite.

In the closing part of his letter he leaves local colour behind and turns to his reading, for which his appetite is every bit as remarkable as his breakfast. He quotes from Corneille's *Le Cid*, Racine's *Phèdre*, Théophile Gautier's *Le Capitaine Fracasse* and makes a play on words drawn from Molière's *Le Bourgeois gentilhomme*; he mentions having read Balzac's *Eugénie Grandet* ('very beautiful, very sad'); he has been studying his Latin, Greek and History; he has read 66 pages of Hugo (which text, we do not know); and produced commentary on 'at least 250 lines of the *Aeneid*'. This remarkable diet – classical, canonical and contemporary – is impressive, particularly for a fifteen-year-old. He ends with comments on the weather, and even this banality has its own sparkle: I would correct my errors of grammar and style, he says, but '*Fé tro cho pour sla*' (*fait trop chaud pour cela* – 's too 'ot for that; *Corr.*, XXI, 543–5). There is an appetite here, a vigorous engagement with the world and with words, which is now opinionated, now mannered, self-regarding and playful. Richard Ellman, the critic and biographer of Wilde, Yeats and Joyce, wrote that 'the pursuit of the finished man in the child is irresistible for us'; when faced with verbal compositions of this sort by a teenaged Proust, the temptation to yield to that impulse is strong indeed.[3]

The letter quoted above gives a sense of the breadth of his reading in fiction and theatre. Around this time he was also captivated by the writing of Augustin Thierry, whose *The Conquest of England by the Normans* (1825) he had been given during a trip to Illiers in the autumn of 1886 occasioned by the death of Adrien's older sister, known to Marcel as 'la tante Amiot', a woman with whom he had little contact but whose somewhat reclusive life above the family shop in Illiers contributed in some measure to the captivating hypochondriac Tante Léonie of Combray. As his parents tended to the details of his aunt's papers, Marcel sat for hours immersed in Thierry's novelistic narrative. He would then go out into the fields around Illiers and experience the stimuli of the outside world with an acuity vastly amplified by the contrast of his new surroundings to his prior enclosed, sedentary state. In drafts for scenes in 'Combray', Proust describes this experience, naming Thierry as the reading matter that left him 'like a wound top'. In the finished novel Thierry's book is not named, but the important, instructive scene remains, where prolonged cerebral engagement leaves the narrator hyper-sensitized to the sights and sounds of the world into which he is then unleashed. He sees the reflection of sunlight across a pond and on the surface of a wall, 'a pallid smile responding to the smiling sky' and inarticulately he cries out '*Zut, zut, zut, zut.*' Crucially, however, he recognizes that he 'was in duty bound not to content [himself] with these un-illuminating words, but to endeavour to see more clearly into the sources of [his] rapture' (*Swann's Way*, 186; I, 153). And this compulsion to achieve a deeper understanding of his relation to the world, identified by the teenage Proust one autumn afternoon, is an important kernel of curiosity from which the mature novel grows.

From Proust's years at Condorcet, many of the reports from his teachers have survived. Although they are never quite as detailed as the fifteen-year-old's report to his grandmother on the *menu du jour* at Salies, they do nevertheless allow us to plot, to some degree,

Marcel's progress. The spring and summer terms, for a hay fever sufferer, were always the most problematic. In Marcel's second year, for the second term his literature teacher, Monsieur Legouëz, notes 'absent for three weeks' and in the third term simply 'absent since May'. Another teacher sympathetically (and perhaps optimistically) notes 'Illness is troubling his work. Good pupil. With health will come success.'[4] That year he was awarded the second prize for Natural Sciences: an impressive achievement if we consider that due to his absences Proust's name does not even feature on the class lists for the third term. By his final year at Condorcet, however, his scientific interest seems to have waned, his physics and chemistry teacher noting: 'Does absolutely nothing.'[5] Despite his absences, Marcel made it through his first three years at the *lycée* largely unhindered; but when he began his fourth year in October 1885 his health had diminished: 'always absent' was the bald summary from his History and Geography teacher in the first term.

In late 1886 or 1887 Proust completed a questionnaire about himself; his answers are intriguing for what they reveal of his character and preoccupations. A trend of the time was for children to have keepsake books, albums in which they made notes and kept records of their activities. Antoinette Faure's keepsake book was printed with questionnaires in English (fashionably) and it was here that Marcel recorded answers (in French) that reveal him to be thoughtful, idealistic and still very much attached to his mother. His favourite occupation? 'Reading, daydreaming, poetry, history, theatre'; where would he like to live? 'In the realm of the ideal, or rather of my ideal'; his idea of misery? 'To be separated from Maman.'[6] The pastimes are much as we would expect from the sickly child from a well-to-do family; the last answer quoted is a reminder of the steadfast bond between mother and son, one that Proust would make particularly prominent in the early parts of *A la recherche*, above all in the scene of the 'bedtime drama' but also much later in the Venice section of *Albertine disparue*. If, with Ellmann, we seek evidence of the 'finished man' in the youthful Proust's answers, perhaps most revealing of all is his response to the question 'For what fault do you have most toleration?' To this Marcel noted '*Pour la vie privée des génies*' (for the private lives of geniuses). This extraordinary answer suggests that already at this young age Proust had developed an understanding that in creative individuals, the 'self' that writes or paints or composes may function (indeed, may exist) at a different level to, as Yeats put it, the 'bundle of accident and incoherence that sits down to breakfast'.[7] As Jean-Yves Tadié has noted, Proust's brief answer contains 'all of *Contre Sainte-Beuve*, an anticipation, a confession, a programme, an aesthetic'.[8] But before the writer could properly emerge from within *petit Marcel*, he had to complete his schooling and work out how to survive in a world where he would, inevitably, be separated from his mother and in which his 'private life' might not be tolerated as magnanimously as his youthful self may have hoped.

Proust's reading, writing and rest put him in a strong position to pick up his studies once more on his return to the *lycée* in October 1886. With his asthma less debilitating, Proust was able more fully to participate in the life of the school. As well as doing the work required of him, he contributed to a number of short-lived reviews that were set up and run by a small group of like-minded pupils. The driving force behind these, first *Le Lundi*, in 1887, then the *Revue de seconde*, the *Revue verte* and the *Revue lilas* (named after the coloured paper on which they were produced), was Proust's new classmate Daniel Halévy. A number of the contributors to these little magazines would be friends to Proust throughout his *lycée* career and beyond, and would go on to achieve considerable literary standing of their own: Halévy became a renowned historian and biographer (notably of Nietzsche and Michelet); Robert Dreyfus was also a historian and, for many years, wrote for *Le Figaro*; Robert de Flers was a prolific playwright and Fernand

Gregh a successful poet and critic; unlike Proust, both Flers and Gregh were elected to the Académie Française.

While the other boys had ambition and ability, Proust, older by a year and a prodigious manipulator of the written and spoken word, even at sixteen commanded their respect in matters intellectual. By the end of his fourth year, Marcel had won second prizes in History and Geography and was put forward to participate in the prestigious *concours général*, the public examinations held at the Sorbonne that pitted against each other the top *lycée* students in the country from each year group. He won no accolades in the *concours* but was admired by his classmates; they were not always entirely reverential, however: Fernand Gregh described how Marcel's exaggeration, simpering and flattery led the boys to coin the verb *proustifier* (to proustify), 'to express an attitude of kindness that is slightly too self-conscious, combined with . . . interminable and delightful affectations'.[9] As time went by Proust's interest in his classmates became frequently and increasingly libidinal (in particular in relation to Jacques Bizet, another of the little circle of friends, the son of Georges Bizet, the composer of *Carmen*), which led to various fallings out and misunderstandings. Proust had enjoyed the companionship of the young girls with whom he played in the Champs-Elysées, but from the letters that have survived from his sixteenth year it is possible to distinguish a clear shift in the nature and focus of his attentions.

In the spring of 1888 Marcel wrote to Jacques Bizet, expressing his 'need for [Bizet's] friendship'. 'I have many troubles', he asserted, continuing somewhat ambiguously, 'Do you want to be my reservoir?' 'My only consolation when I am really sad', he goes on, 'is to love and to be loved. And it is really you who answers to this need' (*Corr.*, XXI, 554). Presumably unsuccessful in his plea, Marcel subsequently took a more direct route, passing his friend a letter, as William Carter puts it, 'inviting him to have sex'.[10] Bizet declines once more, and Proust's response merits quoting for its lyricism (and persistence): 'I find it sad not to pluck the delicious flower, which soon we will no longer be able to pluck. For it will be fruit . . . And forbidden' (*Corr.*, I, 102). Bizet, it seems, was still not interested, but this did not dissuade Marcel, who takes yet another tack in a later letter. Addressing Bizet as '*chéri*' (my dear), Proust writes of his 'somewhat excessive affection' for him, wondering if Bizet has 'the same faults as me (independent mind, nervousness, disordered mind; maybe even masturbation)'. With this part confession, part come-on, any caution he might have thought advisable is thrown to the wind and he informs Bizet that his father had found him masturbating that morning and 'begged him to stop for at least four days' (*Corr.*, XXI, 554–5). Proust suggests that this might have been possible had Bizet agreed to his previous requests for intimacy but now he is left alone, rebuffed by his beau and chided by his cruel, uncomprehending parents.

Around the same time, in a letter to Daniel Halévy, Proust holds forth on the question of homosexuality (the word in common use by the boys was pederasty, which did not have for them the specific meaning in does in English today). 'I know', he writes,

> that there are young men . . . guys aged between eight and seventeen years old, who *love* other guys, who always want to see them (like me, Bizet), who weep and suffer when they are apart from them and want only one thing: to embrace them and put them on their knees, who love them for their *flesh*, who devour them with their eyes, who call them 'my dear', 'my angel', quite seriously, who write them passionate letters and who wouldn't for anything in the world practise pederasty.
>
> However, generally love gets the better of them and they masturbate together. But don't you make fun of them . . . They are, in the end, people who are in love. And I don't know why their love is more unclean than normal love [*je ne sais pas pourquoi leur amour est plus malpropre que l'amour habituel*]. (*Corr.*, XXI, 553)

Marcel's defence of a forbidden sort of love here may be self-serving but is also passionate and principled; it foreshadows, particularly in the last sentence, a trait of the voice that speaks to us in *A la recherche du temps perdu*: its ability to remind us, as Malcolm Bowie has put it, of 'the straightforwardness of non-straight sex'.[11]

Such relations, however, were not openly accepted in French *fin-de-siècle* society. Proust's parents were aware of Marcel's proclivities and sought a 'solution'. It was not uncommon at the time for adolescent boys to visit prostitutes for initiation into the ways of the flesh; and so, hopeful that Marcel would desist from masturbating (and perhaps from further advances on his classmates), his father furnished him with a 10-franc note and sent him in the right direction. In the event, Marcel's nerves got the better of him and he broke a chamber pot in the brothel, for which the proprietors charged him three francs. In his resulting fluster he was not able to perform. These details are preserved for posterity in an extraordinary letter Marcel wrote to his grandfather, explaining what happened and requesting a discreet loan of the necessary funds to complete the transaction without his father finding out what happened at the first attempt.

Other letters from this period shed further light on Proust's intellect and psychological development. On the one hand we can discern the remarkably incisive, critical voice of he whom the editor of Proust's juvenilia has called the young 'Professor of Style'. Yet, on the other hand, letters to his parents and to his closest friends at Condorcet (Halévy, Bizet and Dreyfus) reveal insecurities and a yearning for acceptance, together with complex self-analysis. Proust's marginal notes on a poem sent to him for consideration by Halévy are often brutal ('Formless', 'Idiotic', 'Atrocious').[12] He senses that the piece is a bad copy of decadent writing: something to be avoided. He advises his friend to read (among many others) Homer, Plato, Shakespeare, Descartes, Flaubert, Baudelaire . . . thus, he suggests, the budding poet – by now surely dispirited –

'will learn that if your mind is original and strong your works will be so only if you write with absolute sincerity'. Involuntary pastiche is to be avoided, Proust writes: 'simplicity', he states sagely, with the confidence of an old hand, 'has infinite forms of elegance, and what is natural has unspeakable charm'.[13]

Weighing words and judging the effectiveness of literary expression came easily to Proust. Less evident were his relations with his friends who would tease and torment him in various ways when they grew weary of his propositions and tiresome *proustification*. Once, both Halévy and Bizet stopped talking to and even acknowledging Proust for a whole month. In a plangent letter to Robert Dreyfus, in August 1888 we find Marcel thinking out loud: 'What do they want with me?' he asks. 'To get rid of me, to annoy me, to mystify me, or what? I found them so nice!' (*Corr.*, I, 105–6). Although there is a note of despair in the letter, one also senses, as so often in Proust's correspondence, a palliative pleasure in the very act of writing. 'Excuse my writing, my style, my spelling', he asks of Dreyfus, 'I don't dare reread my words when I write at such a gallop. I do know that one shouldn't write like that. But I've so much to say. It surges forward like waves' (*Corr.*, I, 106). Desire, love, hormonally charged adolescent urges: all these are hard to corral; but when Marcel has pen in hand, expansiveness is no threat – it is a freedom and a comfort. One month later, quite out of the blue, Halévy starts speaking to Proust again. Desperate to understand what motivated his exclusion, he writes again to Dreyfus, using a sort of painstaking calculus to determine the various possible reasons for their actions: it could have been simply a playful game; or a test of the resilience of his friendship; or it could be genuine antipathy, in which case their apparent reconciliation is meaningless. Nuanced processes of mind underpin these various hypotheses and in expressing them to Dreyfus, the seventeen-year-old Proust writes of 'the different individuals of whom I am constituted', each of whom reads a different motivation into his being ignored by his friends (*Corr.*, I, 113). This notion again underscores Proust's growing sense that the self is not monolithic but multiple.

If Proust's intermittent isolation from his friends (for reasons just discussed and because of his fragile health) led him to reflect more than most on identity and his relations to those around him, then embarking on his last year at Condorcet provided him with a new source of stimulus and solace. Alphonse Darlu (1849–1922), his philosophy master, was an exceptional teacher with a redoubtable intellect, and was enormously popular with his pupils. Darlu's first class made such an impression on Proust that he was prompted to write a letter to the master, seeking a 'moral consultation'; and it glows with intellectual candour: 'when I began, at about fourteen or fifteen years old, to withdraw into myself and to study my inner life it was not painful: quite the opposite. Later, around sixteen, it became intolerable, above all physically: it gave me an extreme fatigue, a sort of obsession.' Now, with improved health, Marcel writes, he is better able to cope with the exhaustion and despair that are caused by '*ce dédoublement constant*' (this constant doubling; *Corr.*, I, 119). What he pinpoints in his condition is a suffering that has become 'intellectualized':

I can no longer find complete pleasure in what used to be my supreme joy – literature. When I read, for example, a poem by Leconte de Lisle, while I taste the infinite pleasures of the past, the other *me* considers me, amuses himself in considering the causes of my pleasure, sees them in a certain relation between me and the work, above all imagines immediately opposed conditions of beauty, kills, in the end, almost all of my pleasure . . . To cure myself, all I can do is destroy my inner life, or rather this gaze that is perpetually fixed on my inner life, and this seems to me quite terrifying. (*Corr.*, I, 120)

His experience of crisis is laid bare, the letter classed in its closing lines as 'a sort of confession'. One can imagine the cathartic effect of writing these words: Proust evidently sensed that finally he had identified an interlocutor equipped to appreciate his predicament.

Darlu's class was not plain sailing (one of Proust's essays came back from the master with the miserable mark of four out of twenty, annotated across the first page 'Extremely vague and superficial'); but the study of philosophy, the challenges and the intellectual dynamism that Darlu brought to this new pursuit contributed to Proust's *not* closing his eyes to his inner life. Indeed, the notion first mobilized in the letter to Darlu of the inward-turned gaze is triumphantly reinscribed in one of the clinching images of *Le Temps retrouvé*, where Proust's narrator voices the realization that 'what we have not had to decipher, to elucidate by our own efforts, what was clear before we looked at it, is not ours. From ourselves comes only that which we pull from the obscurity which lies within us, that which to others is unknown' (*Time Regained*, 234; IV, 459). The inward turn would provide riches beyond the young Proust's expectations.

Marcel's health remained more stable than it had been for some time; the group of friends continued with their little magazines; Proust increasingly visited the theatre. He ultimately completed his final year at Condorcet with considerable exit velocity, receiving the top prize in his class for the *dissertation française*. Darlu's tutelage might have helped Proust begin to recognize the potential riches of his inner life but just as his time at the *lycée* was drawing to a close another world – the glittering social world of belle époque Paris – was drawing his attentions in an opposing direction.

In the years immediately following Proust's final term at Condorcet, his social circle expanded rapidly: in the summer of 1889 he was introduced to Mme Arman de Caillavet, who was the mistress of Anatole France, one of the contemporary writers Marcel most

The adolescent Proust photographed by Paul 'Nadar', 1887.

admired. She would receive up to one hundred guests at her Sunday receptions, her salon representing an extraordinary who's who of artists, politicians, diplomats, actors and writers, including many of those whom Proust had read with such enthusiasm in recent years, such as Pierre Loti, Leconte de Lisle and, of course, France himself. Jacques Bizet may have spurned Marcel's amorous attention but this did not preclude him from presenting Proust to his mother, Geneviève Straus. While his tendency to exaggerate and fuss frustrated his classmates, his erudition, wit and the readiness of his compliments soon made him a popular guest at Mme Straus' fashionable salon. Born Geneviève Halévy in 1849, Mme Straus' father was Fromental Halévy, the composer of *La Juive* (*The Jewess*, 1835), one of the nineteenth century's most popular operas. Her cousin, Ludovic Halévy – father of Proust's schoolmate Daniel – was a novelist and, with Henri Meilhac, the librettist for many of Offenbach's popular operettas (such as *La Belle Hélène* and *Barbe-bleue*). Geneviève married the composer Georges Bizet when she was twenty and gave birth to Jacques in 1872. She had lost her father when she was thirteen, her sister and her mother when she was fifteen and then, in 1875, just a few months after Bizet's *Carmen* was met most unfavourably by audiences and critics alike, she lost her husband to a heart attack and became a widow at twenty-six. Geneviève was beautiful, cultured and intelligent, but her accumulated woes and nervous disposition left her often depressed. This temperament notwithstanding, she was, like Oriane de Guermantes in Proust's novel, a consummate hostess and famous for her witticisms. In 1886 she married Emile Straus, a wealthy lawyer with an admirable art collection, including a notable number of Monets. With Emile's contacts, Geneviève's verve and her artistic pedigree, composers, painters and 'people of talent' commingled *chez* Straus with the aristocrats of Saint-Germain. It was there that Proust first encountered the denizens of the beau monde; in particular, he met Charles Haas (1832–1902), the epitome of worldly sophistication and panache. Jewish, handsome, wealthy, an acquaintance of poets (such as Montesquiou) and artists (such as Degas), lover of Sarah Bernhardt, and a member of the Jockey Club, France's most exclusive members club, Haas was someone to whom *A la recherche*'s Charles Swann bears more than a passing resemblance. Through acquaintances Marcel made *chez* Straus and Mme de Caillavet, invitations to other salons came his way. When he started seeking a publisher for his novel in 1912, the reputation he had by then developed as a socialite and a dilettante (rather than as a 'serious' author) proved difficult to shake off.

In July 1889, just a fortnight before the Condorcet prize-giving, as visitors to the Exposition Universelle thronged the machine galleries and marvelled at the great tower of iron soaring above them, the French government voted in a law that ended the regime of voluntary, one-year service and instigated obligatory enlistment for three years. There was, however, a grace period incorporated: those *volunteering* during this time could still sign up for just one year, rather than three. Before enlisting, Marcel took a break in Ostende with the family of a Condorcet friend, Horace Finaly. He was miserable rather than jubilant, though, separated from his mother, who was holidaying with Robert at Salies-de-Béarn. Her daily letters (to 'My poor dear little wolf') betray fears about her son's well-being that one might expect to be provoked by an absent child, rather than a young man. 'Could you please date each of your letters', requests Mme Proust:

> I will be able to follow things more easily. Then tell me
>> Got up at –
>> Went to bed at –
>> Hours of fresh air –
>> Hours of rest –
>> Etc.
> The statistics will have their own eloquence for me and in just a few lines you will have fulfilled your duties. (*Corr.*, 1, 129)

The intelligent, gifted school leaver, budding socialite, soon to be army recruit, was still happy to behave, and to be treated, like a child.

Crowds walking under the base of the Eiffel Tower during the Exposition Universelle, 1889.

Proust enlisted for his year's *voluntariat* on 11 November 1889; he was attached to the first battalion of the 76th Infantry Regiment, based at the Coligny Barracks in the city of Orléans, about 80 miles southwest of Paris. His weight was not entered on his service record, but he is listed as just 1 m 68 cm (5 ft 6 in) tall; his hair and eyes are 'chestnut', his chin rounded, his mouth and eyes 'average'. Soon after moving into the barracks he was moved out again: his nocturnal coughing fits were too much for the other recruits. The officers, turning a blind eye to the regulations, lodged Proust privately nearby in Orléans. As a result, although again in contravention of the rules, he was able to entertain friends for dinner in these quarters, where they enjoyed wines sent by Professor and Mme Proust in more comfortable surroundings than were provided on base.

Although Proust's letters to his mother from this period have not survived, some of Mme Proust's have: written with great regularity, they are tender, concerned and reassuring. Every Sunday, Marcel had leave and almost without fail he would return by an early morning train to the Gare d'Austerlitz so as to maximize the hours he could spend with his mother. Fearing that the separation was getting too much for him after just one month away from home, Mme Proust proposed a coping strategy of the sort one might offer a child, based on consuming a bar of chocolate on the last day of each month: 'you'll be astonished to see how they fly by – and with them your exile', she writes (*Corr.*, I, 134), the vocabulary of exile underlining that Mme Proust clearly felt that her son's rightful place was in close proximity to her at home. Professor Proust's contact with his son was tenuous. His wife would pass on messages, usually health-related: in one letter horse riding and swimming are discouraged, as is the excessive consumption of crème cheese. Overall, it seems that thanks to various indulgences from well-disposed superiors, tactical evasions and fortunate turns of events that worked in his favour, Proust managed to scrape, or dodge, his way through his training without any major setbacks. At the final classification of his cohort, Proust ranked 63rd of 64 recruits.

He enjoyed the sociability of his period of service and recalled it warmly in later years. It allowed him to mix with a diverse range of male companions from a variety of social strata; he could listen, observe, compare. He met men of *ancien régime* nobility, such as the officer to whom he answered directly, Comte Armand-Pierre de Cholet; he also encountered men of more recent title, the Noblesse d'Empire, such as Comte Charles Colonna-Walewski, a grandson of Napoleon Bonaparte; and he absorbed the nuances of their respective attitudes and foibles. This sociological fieldwork nourishes *A la recherche* in a number of ways, most obviously in *The Guermantes Way* when the narrator goes to the barracks in Doncières to visit his friend Saint-Loup (whose lineage is very much that of Cholet rather than Walewski).

A little less than two months into Proust's military service, his maternal grandmother died. Proust had been able to see Adèle Weil in December when he was on leave, but by then she was already gravely ill. When she died on 3 January 1890 (from uraemia, the condition that would also take Marcel's mother), Proust was already back in Orléans. He attended the funeral on 5 January, but it seems that he did not come to terms with his loss for some time. In a letter from Mme Proust in June it is clear that Marcel has recently explained that he has not been writing because he did not wish to increase his mother's grief by sharing with her his own. In Proust's novel, the narrator has a displaced experience of mourning, appreciating only belatedly his grandmother's passing when an involuntary flood of emotion overwhelms him as he repeats an action (loosening his boots) that she had helped him with long before; he describes this retroactive realization as 'the intermittences of the heart', a phrase that, for a time, Proust considered using as the overall title of his novel. The death of the narrator's grandmother in *A la recherche* is one of the most touching moments in the novel. Proust did not witness Adèle Weil's death, however: in constructing the pages relating the fictional grandmother's final illness and death in *The Guermantes Way*, Proust drew on his experience of witnessing his mother's final days in 1905 as well as his grief at the loss of his grandmother. The emotive force of his fiction, we might say, is what we gain from his double experience of loss.

Proust's completion of his schooling, his military service and the death of his grandmother are all events that one might expect to have precipitated or at least encouraged a more developed sense of independence. It is not possible to judge for sure whether or not this was the case. Mme Proust's letters from August 1890 repeatedly voice complaints about Marcel's lack of correspondence. At the end of the month she demands of him an 'act of contrition': he

Proust during his military service, 1889–90.

should buy sufficient paper and envelopes to be able to send her '60 letters, which will be most agreeable', effectively one per day for the remainder of his time at Orléans. These are hardly the actions of a mother encouraging the autonomy of her son; Marcel, however, was not exactly straining at the leash. A letter to his father at the end of his service remarks that the 'general melancholy' that had hung over him for the last year, caused or at least explicable by 'his absence [from home]', seems to have lifted now that his return is imminent (*Corr.*, I, 159). In mid-November 1890, then, Private Proust was discharged from service; and *petit Marcel* returned to the family home to contemplate the road ahead.

## 3

# Undergraduate, Critic, Duellist

What are the secret relations, the necessary metamorphoses that exist between the life of a writer and his work, between reality and art, or rather, as we thought at that time, between the appearances of life and the reality itself which was their lasting basis and which art brought into relief?[1]

Returning to Paris, the barracks room and the parade square gave way to the comforts and pleasures of boulevard Malesherbes and the society salons; wing-collar shirts, Liberty-print ties and evening dress soon ousted kepi and greatcoat. But the transition from military to civilian life was more than a change of surroundings and a change of dress. It was time to think – and make decisions – about a career. The word *carrière*, evidently one that cast an ominous shadow for Proust in his early twenties, recurs with increasing, panicked frequency in his letters of the period between 1891 and 1896. His parents were keen for him to enrol for a course of studies that would lead him into the diplomatic service; writing was assuredly what interested him most, but in his parents' eyes this was not a *career*. In the period between the end of his service at Orléans in late 1890 and January 1897, when his name was published among the signatories to the 'Intellectuals' Manifesto' in support of the plight of Alfred Dreyfus, Proust's activity was concentrated in three areas: his university studies, his ever-increasing social engagements and his first steps as a published writer. Proust did not shine particularly as a student, nor did he cement his status as one of the finest writers of his generation at this time: his great novel would not properly begin to take shape for another decade, around 1908. The 1890s were vital, however, in the shaping of Marcel's faculties: developing the modulation and tone of his critical and creative voices, attuning his ear and refining the scope and acuity of his already extraordinary vision. He half-heartedly studied for and was awarded two *licence* (bachelor's) degrees; he whole-heartedly attended receptions, dinners, concerts, opera and the theatre. In a variety of journals and newspapers he published reviews, articles and short prose sketches, and many of these were published together in his first book, *Les Plaisirs et les jours* (*Pleasures and Days*) in 1896. His health problems continued: his breathing troubles and inability to sleep are unbroken threads through the correspondence with his mother. He experienced the loss of contemporaries in their youth (Willie Heath to dysentery and Edgar Aubert to acute appendicitis) and of his grandfather and great uncle in old age. These reminders of mortality came interleaved with the exhilarations and disillusions brought about with the pendulum swings of desire, above all for Reynaldo Hahn and Lucien Daudet. The music of Saint-Saëns, Massenet and Wagner filled Proust's ears and his eyes and mind absorbed Tolstoy, Balzac and George Eliot. Throughout these years the young man sought substance for his art and a means of expressing his relation to the reality surrounding him. His responses – critical essays; tales of jealousy and betrayal; sighing, lyrical reflections; social critiques and character sketches; disparate draft scenes for a novel – are not masterpieces but they set vital processes in motion, begin 'necessary metamorphoses' and promise, now with confidence, now in a filigree of shadows or whispers, the shape of things to come.

Almost immediately that he returned to Paris, Proust began contributing to *Le Mensuel*, a monthly review sold from a small number of bookshops in the eighth arrondissement between October 1890 and September 1891. Proust wrote on a variety of topics (from poetry and fashion to reviews of popular theatre and contemporary music hall, including performances at the famous Folies-Bergère and the Ambassadeurs). He wrote under a range of pseudonyms, some playful ('Pierre de Touche', Touch Stone) and some less so ('Bob'). 'Choses normandes' (Things of Normandy) was the first piece to be signed 'Marcel Proust' and appeared in *Le Mensuel*'s final issue. In it, Proust evokes the landscapes and the effects of light peculiar to Normandy (he had stayed in Cabourg and Trouville for a spell at the end of the summer of 1891). This short piece, focusing on the sensory riches of the coastal setting, the motif of the '*soleil rayonnant sur la mer*' (the sun shining on the sea, a phrase from 'Chant d'automne', 'Autumn Song', a poem in Baudelaire's *Les Fleurs du mal*), and the bewitching perspectival play of land and sea, anticipates *Within a Budding Grove*, Balbec and the lessons Proust's narrator learns there from the painter Elstir.

The trip that fuelled this short article was a holiday marking the end of Proust's first year at the Sorbonne and the Ecole Libre des Sciences Politiques. The combined study of law and political science was a common trajectory for high-achieving sons of wealthy families destined for the diplomatic service. Proust's professors at the Ecole Libre were leaders in their field: Albert Sorel, who succeeded Hippolyte Taine in the Académie Française in 1894, was in the midst of his influential, eight-volume *L'Europe et la révolution française* (1885–1904); Albert Vandal was a historian specializing in the Orient, elevated to the Académie in 1896; and Anatole Leroy-Beaulieu wrote widely on Russia, socialism and religion. Proust may not have been a model student (he took few lecture notes, preferring to pass distracting scribbles to his companions) but he was exposed to the vast learning of these scholars and to expansive critical vocabularies that would enrich (often humorously) his future novel, above all through the repartee of characters such as the diplomat Norpois and the academic Brichot.

The artist as a young man, portrait by Jacques-Emile Blanche, 1892, oil on canvas.

Jacques-Emile Blanche made a pencil sketch of Proust at
Trouville in October 1891; early the following year when Proust
sat for the painter, on a succession of Saturday mornings in his
studio in Auteuil, it was as a socialite that Blanche captured
him in oils and this image has proved to be remarkably enduring
(Blanche referred to his sitter at this time as 'an apprentice dandy').[2]
Proust's hair is sleek and neatly parted, his skin ghostly pale, fine
brows arching over deep, searching eyes and pursed lips, the very

Proust serenades Jeanne Pouquet at the Boulevard Bineau tennis courts, Neuilly-sur-Seine, 1892.

muted background only just permitting the viewer to discern the dark outlines of his evening dress, but forming a contrast all the sharper with the sensuous outline of the white lily in his buttonhole. The Proust of Blanche's portrait is handsome, yet delicate; he holds our gaze and gives little away. Laure Hayman, who remained an object of Proust's flattering attention, called him her 'little porcelain psychologist' because of his incisive talk and the pallor of his skin.

In the summer of 1891 his friend Gaston de Caillavet, son of Mme Arman, whose salon Proust had recently started to attend, spent much spare time playing tennis at the new courts on the Boulevard Bineau in Neuilly. Proust would attend, but refused to play 'so violent a game' and preferred to sit at the side with the young girls and mothers who gathered in the shade and liked to listen to his conversation.[3] One of these *jeunes filles* was Jeanne Pouquet, whom Proust adored and who would marry Gaston in April 1893. Proust acted as Gaston's best man, but during the time of the trend for tennis he almost ruined their friendship with his insistent requests for a photograph of Jeanne, something Gaston was not willing to supply. Proust's yearning for photographs with which to create a sort of personal archive, a set of memories that would never fade, was a constant throughout his adult life. Over and again in his correspondence we find him trying to get his hands on such mementos. This fetishistic attachment to snapshots (one shared by Proust's narrator in *A la recherche*) captured the imagination of director Raoul Ruiz, who opens his filmic interpretation of *Time Regained* (1999) with the aged, bed-bound writer poring over photographs that loom in and out of focus under his quavering magnifying glass. Little could be further from this poignant image of the aged writer than the photo that has survived of Proust from 1892, a carefree young man kneeling at the feet of Jeanne Pouquet, herself standing atop a chair at the tennis courts, Proust with a tennis racket grasped like a guitar, braced for an adoring serenade.

The simple juxtaposition of Blanche's man-about-town and the impish faux-crooner of the tennis courts reminds us again of the multiplicity of Proust's character. At once student, socialite and budding writer, he displays a constantly shifting palate of adult and childish characteristics. Fernand Gregh remarked on this trait, noting that 'at first he seems to be no more than a handsome young boy; but when he speaks his eyes shine with a brightness that luminously gilds all the traits of his face.'[4] Almost immediately after completing his military service, Marcel's gilded visage was gracing Mme Straus' salon. He sent her flowers (chrysanthemums, a variety new to France and one for which Odette Swann would have a particular fondness) and wrote to her assiduously, as if each successive letter was in competition with the extravagant flatteries of the last. There is something childish about the excessiveness of Proust's flattery, the lack of constraint in his verbal effusions, yet this childishness is held in tension with the mature qualities of intelligence, astuteness and irony that underpin his outpourings.

Laure Hayman, as well as Mme Straus, received Marcel's missives; but his idolatry was not confined to his female correspondents. He met Comte Robert de Montesquiou-Fezensac in April 1893 *chez* Madeleine Lemaire, another hostess (and amateur painter of flowers) with whom he had become acquainted, and the idiosyncratic aristocrat-poet, who had served as the model for Des Esseintes, the protagonist of Huysmans' *A rebours* (*Against Nature*, 1884), immediately had the young Proust magnetized. That summer, upon receipt of an advance copy of a collection of Montesquiou's poems, Proust wrote the count a letter of thanks whose postscript likened the poet to 'a firmament of stars' and himself to an 'earth worm' (*Corr.*, I, 213). We recognize now, however, that it is the lowly worm that shines with a resolute brightness in the modern literary firmament, while Montesquiou is remembered, if at all, as a minor poet, an emblem of decadent excess.

During his military service Proust met Robert de Billy, a serious, intelligent young man two years his senior. Billy was not impressed: as he put it, '[Proust's] movement and his speech did not conform to the military ideal'.[5] But the way Proust spoke of art and of his philosophy teacher Darlu made an impression, and when the two met again a few months later at the Ecole Libre, civilians once more, they were instantly friends. Outside class Proust and de Billy would visit the Louvre, Proust reciting from memory lines of Baudelaire's 'Les Phares' ('The Guiding Lights'), as they looked at works by the painters mentioned in the poem (later, *Pleasures and Days* would include a section of poems, 'Portraits of Painters', whose genesis stems from these visits).

Another major stimulus for Proust's writing of this period came from his being part of a group of old classmates from Condorcet (Fernand Gregh, who was chief editor, Jacques Bizet, Robert Dreyfus, Horace Finaly, Daniel Halévy and Louis de la Salle), who founded a literary review entitled *Le Banquet*, after the French title for Plato's *Symposium*. Thanks to Bizet's contact with the director of the newspaper *Le Temps* they were able to have the journal professionally printed. It ran through eight issues between 1892 and 1893; although the circulation was relatively small, the journal is a fascinating window on the preoccupations of a talented group of budding writers. The editors' notice in the first edition nails their ambitions to the mast: they want to see their work in print, but they also wish 'to make known in France, in a sustained way,

Mr Marcel Proust, Editor: calling card for *Le Banquet*, 1892.

the most recent and most interesting productions of foreign art.'
'The breadth of our eclecticism', they write, 'will reconcile our
temperaments.'[6] And eclectic the subsequent numbers proved
to be: we find the translation of a fragment of Ibsen's *Emperor
and Galilean* (1873) by Daniel Halévy; excerpts from Nietzsche's
*Beyond Good and Evil* (1886) translated into French for the first
time by Halévy and Fernand Gregh; as well as original poems
and prose sketches; translations from Swinburne and Dante
Gabriel Rossetti; and, in the penultimate number for February
1893, Proust's first extended fictional narrative, 'Violante; ou, la
mondanité' ('Violante; or, Worldly Vanities'), to which I will return.

In January 1892 Proust's cousin Louise Neuberger married the
philosopher Henri Bergson. Born in 1859, Bergson had excelled in
mathematics and philosophy at Condorcet, took up a place at the
Ecole Normale Supérieure in 1878, taught philosophy in a number
of provincial schools before ascending to the heights of the *lycée*
Henri-IV in Paris and, in 1900, a chair at the Collège de France,
where his public lectures drew vast crowds. Bergson explored the
human experience of time as a fluid, flowing *durée*, or duration, in
contrast to the artificial divisions we habitually impose on time in
order to make it measurable; he also explored the role of memory
in the perennial tension between mind and body in the act of
perception. Even these schematic sketches of Bergson's rich,
often lyrical investigations into the nature of our being in the
world give a sense of their proximity to Proust's own philosophico-
literary concerns. What is remarkable, though, is the fact that the
two men never exchanged ideas at any length. The extant letters
between them are few and unrevealing of any intimacy, intellectual
or otherwise.

Marcel's manners and his entertaining talk were making him
the toast of the salons. Some measure of this can be seen in the
dedication of 'Madame de Luzy', a story in Anatole France's collection
*L'Etui de nacre* (*Mother of Pearl*), published in September 1892. The

dedication was a small thing, but France's reputation was not – he was a sought-after sponsor; that he should dedicate a story to Proust and also deign to write (albeit at Mme Arman's behest) a brief preface for *Pleasures and Days* suggests that he, at least, had some inkling of the earthworm's literary promise. Meanwhile, as Marcel was ingratiating himself to the Paris social elite and doing the bare minimum of work for his law degree, Proust *père*'s tireless endeavours continued, with missions to Spain, to Egypt and to Venice, all in the period from 1890 to 1892. His public service was again formally recognized in December 1892 with his promotion to Commandeur de la Légion d'Honneur.

Around this time Proust completed another questionnaire and his answers are revealing of the development in his character, as well as of those traits, such as his adoring attachment to his mother, that remain the same. As one might expect, his preferred authors have changed: Sand and Thierry, who leave their mark on 'Combray', are ousted by contemporaries Anatole France and Pierre Loti; his favourite poets are now Vigny and Baudelaire. In an answer that indicates Proust's awareness of the demands he makes of others, he notes 'the principal trait of [his] character' as 'the need to be loved and, to be precise, the need to be caressed and spoiled, rather than admired'. What would be his 'greatest sadness'? 'Not to have known [his] mother or [his] grandmother.' Proust's response to the question of his 'principal fault' gives further insight into his developing psyche: '*Ne pas savoir, ne pas pouvoir "vouloir"*' (not to know how, not to be able to 'will').[7] This intriguing formulation is consonant with the concerns about his 'career' voiced throughout the correspondence of this period. It also suggests that Marcel may suffer from 'abulia', a deficiency of willpower, which was thought at the time to be a symptom of neurasthenia. Problems of *volonté* would be addressed in the 1897 book Professor Proust published with his colleague Gilbert Ballet, *L'Hygiène du neurasthénique* (*Treatment of the Neurasthenic*). They had also been explored before in the writings of the psychologist Théodule Ribot, author of a study of Schopenhauer's philosophy in 1874 and a number of popular works on ailments relating to attention, the will, memory and personality. Proust would acknowledge Ribot's 'fine book', *Les Maladies de la volonté* (*Ailments of the Will*), in the 1904 preface to his translation of Ruskin's *Sesame and Lilies*, but remarks in an earlier essay on Montesquiou indicate that he knew Ribot's work in 1894.[8] A weakness or lack of will is a characteristic shared by Proust and the narrator of *A la recherche*; we also find it in the title character of the earlier tale 'Violante; or, Worldly Vanities', which dates from the time of the second questionnaire.

Published in *Le Banquet* in March 1893, this story was written in August–September 1892, a detail that is not without interest for, while Proust was engaged in writing his cautionary moral fable about the false allure of society life, the rest of France was gripped by Zola's *La Débâcle*, a sweeping, fictionalized account of France's defeat at Sedan and the events of the Paris Commune. Mme Proust mentions reading it in a letter to her son in August 1892 (*Corr.*, I, 179) and she was not alone: published two months earlier, *La Débâcle* sold 176,000 copies before the end of the year: enough, if piled one on top of the other, as *Le Figaro* reported, to reach more than eleven times the height of the Eiffel Tower.[9] Proust's writing was not yet evoking the major socio-historical preoccupations of his day ('Violante' includes chapters titled 'Sensuality' and 'Pains of Love'), but he would soon be a committed, active supporter of Alfred Dreyfus, and in time the development of the Dreyfus Affair would be memorably woven into the fabric of *A la recherche*.

A significant step up in Proust's visibility as a writer came in July 1893 with the publication of nine short *études* (prose sketches) in *La Revue blanche*, a highly regarded journal that was, as one commentator has put it, 'a dazzling artistic and intellectual crucible'.[10] Many of these pieces would eventually be incorporated into *Pleasures and Days*, but it was not until early in 1894 that

Calmann-Lévy agreed in principle to publish the book and it was two more years before it appeared. Although his letters in this period regularly record 'horrible asthma attacks' and 'choking fits', Proust's social and literary activity seems to abate very little. He met Princesse Mathilde Bonaparte, cousin of Napoleon III, *chez* Straus and frequented her own rarefied salon from late 1891. Mathilde was 50 years Proust's senior, a monument of the Noblesse d'Empire and in many ways a living incarnation of the past. In July 1893 Proust first set eyes on the Comtesse Greffulhe, née Elisabeth de Caraman-Chimay, a cousin of Montesquiou and a passionate devotee of the arts, particularly Wagner's music. 'I have never seen such a beautiful woman', Proust opined (*Corr.*, I, 217), and indeed a number of photographs of the Comtesse, in elaborate gowns by Worth or Fortuny, bear witness to her considerable charm.

Although he paid homage to the beauty and grace of the doyennes of high society, at heart Proust remained attached to his male acquaintances; and his studies had given him the chance to meet and appreciate a good many handsome young men. Through Robert de Billy he met Edgar Aubert, whose life was cut short by appendicitis in September 1892. Through Aubert he met Willie Heath, an English cousin of Aubert's about whom little is known except that Proust enjoyed his conversation and valued his company enough to grant him the cherished seat next to his mother at a dinner he arranged for friends in June 1893. Heath's constitution was even weaker than Proust's, however, and in October he succumbed to dysentery. Proust wrote the following month to Robert de Billy – whom he had also 'lost' (to the diplomatic service) – and his letter is revealing of the force of his feelings for these two unfortunate young men: 'I am publishing this year a collection of little things, most of which you already know. I immediately had the thought of dedicating this little book to the memory of two beings whom I knew only for a short time but who I loved, who I love with all my heart, Edgar Aubert – and Willie Heath'

(*Corr.*, I, 245). In the event, Aubert's family declined the offer, and when *Pleasures and Days* was published it was dedicated solely to '*Mon ami Willie Heath*'.

In addition to his bereavement, Proust had finally to face up to the question of his career. He had holidayed in St Moritz with Louis de la Salle, spent time in Evian-les-Bains on the shore of Lake Geneva, and then joined his mother in Trouville in September. As time drew on the pressure increased. 'I am in quite the most awkward predicament', he wrote to Robert de Billy in September, 'for I have to decide – Papa commands it – on my career' (*Corr.*, I, 234). With one or two resit exams along the way, he had fulfilled the requirements for his *licence en droit* and would graduate in October. But what then? In a letter to his father later in September he seems to have whittled down his choices to the *concours* for the diplomatic service or for the Ecole des Chartes, which would see him training to become an archivist or librarian. He argues that he would sooner train as a stockbroker than as a lawyer, insisting that it is not the case that he believes that devoting himself to anything other than literature or philosophy would be '*du temps perdu*' (lost/wasted time) 'but among several ills, some are better than others. I've never conceived of anything more atrocious, on my most desperate days, than a lawyer's office. Embassies, by allowing me to avoid the lawyer's office, would seem to me not a vocation, but a remedy' (*Corr.*, I, 236). There seems to have been some sort of compromise, for Marcel did undertake an internship of two weeks at a lawyer's practice after the award of his *licence*. But in December he wrote a great many letters crammed with queries to Charles Grandjean, the librarian of the Sénat, who Proust, doubtless aware that he was testing his correspondent's patience, cloyingly described as a 'dictionary of all human knowledge, of universal tact and intuition' (*Corr.*, I, 259). Eventually a decision was made and Marcel enrolled for a *licence* in philosophy, a further step towards the Ecole des Chartes.

Proust's reading and study for this degree undoubtedly fed his mind and further developed his critical capacities, but even though he was taking private tutorials with Darlu, his correspondence is markedly lacking in the sort of effusiveness about his studies that his *lycée* philosophy year had provoked. His *licence* was certainly not the *temps perdu* that the drudgery of a lawyer's office would have been, but as so often for Proust in his early years, it was not from his 'official' occupation that he drew his primary sustenance. In 1894–95 Marcel made the acquaintance of two young men: Reynaldo Hahn and Lucien Daudet. His fondness for and (inevitably, it seems, with the young Proust) subsequent attraction to them each in turn brought pleasure and turmoil in almost equal measure.

Proust's portrait had been publically exhibited in the summer of 1893; a second set of his *études* had appeared in the *Revue blanche* in December 1893; his first book was nearing completion, and his pen was not drying up. Such accomplishments at a young age (Proust was not quite 23) suggested promise, but were scarcely more impressive than those of Reynaldo Hahn (1874–1947), the handsome, dark-haired musician who met Proust in the salon of Madeleine Lemaire. Born in Caracas to a Venezuelan Catholic mother and a German Jewish father, Hahn's family established itself in Paris in 1877. He began the piano aged five, entered the Paris Conservatoire aged ten, composed his first popular works, settings of Verlaine's *Chansons grises*, between thirteen and sixteen, and when he met Proust was working on *L'Ile du rêve*, an opera based on Pierre Loti's novel *Le Mariage de Loti* (1880), much enjoyed by Marcel and Mme Proust. The two young men had much in common and quickly their mutual admiration and intimacy grew: Proust's first letter to Hahn in July 1894 is addressed '*Cher Monsieur*' (Dear Sir); by September he is addressing Hahn as 'My little Master' (in English and in French) and signing himself off 'your Pony'.

Madeleine Lemaire invited Proust and Hahn to spend August 1894 with her at her country residence, the Château de Réveillon, in the Seine-et-Marne *département*. In a letter to his cousin, Hahn describes Proust as 'ecstatic and dreamy, a boy of the very best sort, a musician vibrating with every disparate harmony like an Aeolian harp'.[11] Hahn revealingly describes Proust in terms of music, what he knows best; and for his part, Proust described Hahn's voice as one that goes straight to the hearts of his audience, 'dampens everyone's eyes, in the shiver of admiration that he spreads and that makes us tremble, bends us all forward one after the other like a hushed and solemn undulation of wheat in the wind' (*CSB*, 463).

During their time at Réveillon, while out walking together, Proust stopped to look at some Bengal roses. Hahn paused too, but Proust insisted he carry on, leaving him alone with the roses. Reynaldo did so, walked around the chateau, and on his return found Proust still at the same spot, his head bent forward, brows slightly furrowed in passionate scrutiny of the delicate flowers before him, the fingers of his left hand constantly worrying at the ends of his moustache. Hahn passed him by once more and only shortly after did Proust break from his contemplation and rejoin his friend, who felt it inappropriate to question him. This was the first of many such scenes that Hahn witnessed, where Proust slipped into a sort of communion 'with nature, with art, with life', bringing his 'superhuman intelligence and sensibility' to bear on whatever caught his eye.[12] Proust's writing was fuelled as much by his time spent in grand salons and dining rooms as it was by moments like this, before the humble hawthorns at Auteuil or the roses at Réveillon.

After Réveillon, Proust went to Trouville, to take the seaside air with his mother. There he worked on three tales that would be the most substantial, sustained narratives in *Pleasures and Days*: 'The Death of Baldassare Silvande', 'The Confession of a Young Girl' and 'The End of Jealousy'. In mid-September Proust wrote to Hahn, whom he was missing, seeking to secure some more time together:

'since Maman will be leaving soon,' writes the 23-year-old, 'you could come after her departure to console me.' As so often, the childlike and adult coexist in this letter, which closes with a postscript, quite unrelated to the body of the letter, accusing Hahn's view of Wagner's *Lohengrin* of being overly severe and speaking up for the opera, which had just seen its 100th performance in Paris (*Corr.*, I, 325). Frequently we find Proust moving quite effortlessly between his affections for his mother and for young men such as Hahn, moves we find in the mature novel, where – somewhat disarmingly – the narrator alludes, for example, to Albertine's kiss and that of his mother in the same breath. In a letter to Hahn during a later separation, Proust goes even further: 'my dear little one, I will be so, so happy when I can embrace you again, you who really are the person who, with Maman, I love the most in the world' (*Corr.*, II, 88). Happiness for Proust did not need to be subdivided or classified into different types: love was love was love.

In the spring of 1895, shortly after learning that he had fulfilled the requirements for his philosophy degree, Proust found himself in what was for him a traumatic situation, leaving a deep impression that would subsequently find fictional form in a similar episode played out between Swann and Odette in 'Swann in Love'. Proust missed an evening appointment with Reynaldo by a very fine margin, held up by the demanding Mme Lemaire. Both Hahn and Proust sought each other out through the Paris streets but their efforts were unrewarded. Proust's characteristic summary of the experience as 'a veritable tragedy, deep and troubling' (*Corr.*, I, 378) suggests that the separation anxieties he experienced in relation to his mother now had a new object in his beloved *petit Maître*.

Love, however, has a habit of fading. After being introduced in December 1894 to Alphonse Daudet (1840–1897), a major figure of nineteenth-century letters, just a few months later Proust met Daudet's sons, Léon, who was five years older than Marcel, and Lucien, who was not yet seventeen and was an embodiment of the youthful beauty that had so powerful an appeal for Proust. His eventual intimacy with Lucien was the cause of conflict, both familial and of a more public sort, ending in a duel fought with pistols against the journalist Jean Lorrain in February 1897. Reynaldo remained an intimate friend and confidant, but in 1896–7 it was Lucien who attracted the greater part of Proust's amorous energies.

His professional energies, such as they were, were channelled in June 1895 into an examination to determine the allocation of three unpaid positions at the Bibliothèque Mazarine. Proust came last. Rather than being posted to the hallowed seventeenth-century reading rooms on the quai de Conti, he was allocated a position in the *dépôt légal*, the rather less romantic book repository on the rue de Grenelle. Not one to be saddled with a task that did not match his expectations, Proust replied to his appointment letter with the suggestion that someone enjoying better health take up the position. When the administrator remarked that 'M. Proust seemed to me to enjoy excellent health' (*Corr.*, 1, 85), Proust took a different tack and countered with a request for a leave of absence on health grounds, bolstered by a supporting letter from his father's friend Gabriel Hanotaux, the Minister for Foreign Affairs. He did in the end work some shifts in a temporary post but was granted two months' leave at the end of July, leave that would be extended ad hoc until March 1900 when he was formally considered as having resigned. Through a combination of indolence, self-centredness and nepotism Proust managed, in the space of a month, to free himself of the millstone of following a parentally sanctioned career. His parents' worries about him would not disappear (his sexual 'inversion' and his health were enough to be going on with), but they did seem to dissipate somewhat, since he had at least gone through the motions of securing employment.

He still spent a good deal of time with Reynaldo in 1895. After a stay with his mother in the spa town of Kreuznach in Germany,

Proust travelled in August to Dieppe with Hahn, where they resided in Madeleine Lemaire's villa. They walked, read, took the air and admired the sea. Reynaldo and Marcel were intent on a trip to Brittany, but Lemaire, possessive and protective of her flock, like Mme Verdurin and her 'little clan', did not want her protégés to leave her, claiming their health might suffer should they stray from her villa's comforts to the untamed wilds of Britanny. Sarah Bernhardt, however, with whom Reynaldo was acquainted, had transformed a Napoleonic Fort on Belle-Ile-en-Mer into her off-shore stronghold, where she held court amid views of the crashing Atlantic waves. The friends crossed the Bay of Biscay to visit her on 4 September, but their stay was short-lived: Proust's stomach troubled him and by 6 September they were back on the mainland. They took in the sights and established themselves in the annex of a small hotel at Beg Meil, which was without even lavatory facilities. Proust, undaunted, did not baulk at this rusticity, although he did discover that 'nothing is so *irritating* as the excessive zeal of nettles' (*Corr.*, I, 425). His time in Brittany allowed for much contemplation of the ever-changing appearance of the sea; and here he began drafting new material, scenes centred on the life of a character called Jean Santeuil. Over the following five years he produced over 1,000 pages of this material, which came to light 30 years after his death, much of it bearing traces of his youth and his experiences at Réveillon and at Beg Meil. Crucially, however, it lacked a coherent plot or overarching structure. These would only come later, with the determining shift from 'Jean' to the '*je*' of *A la recherche*, the first-person voice that defines the work we know today.

A new project was under way, then, but Proust's first book was still not published; he did not receive the proofs for *Pleasures and Days* until March 1896. The end of 1895, however, saw yet more writing, not additions to his first book but critical prose of an insightful and mature sort that retains its acuity today: an essay on the painting of 'Chardin and Rembrandt' and 'Against Obscurity', an essay attacking the unnecessary opacity of symbolist writing and celebrating what he calls the 'latent music' that exists already in language, to which poets ought simply to alert us. The two essays do quite similar things: they suggest that art is about vision, careful scrutiny and balanced exposition, the communication of impressions made on the artist through the use of language, colour and light, rather than the conjuring of aesthetic effects through complex artifice. Chardin's paintings are triumphs because they show us unexpected beauty in the most humble and banal of subjects. And everyday language, properly handled, can buzz with music and semantic riches that are always there, just dulled by overuse. Proust's essay on the two great painters he had seen at the Louvre, turned down by the *Revue hebdomadaire*, was first published posthumously in *Le Figaro* in 1954 (see *ASB*, 122–31; *CSB*, 372–82). 'Against Obscurity' was published by the *Revue blanche* in July 1896 (see *ASB*, 135–9; *CSB*, 390–95), provoking in response one of Mallarmé's finest essays, 'Le Mystère dans les lettres' ('The Mystery in Letters').

Some years later Proust wrote, famously, that an artist's work 'is the product of a self other than that which we display in our habits, in company, in our vices' (*ASB*, 12; *CSB*, 221). This dictum might be illustrated in Proust's own case if we consider the fine essays just discussed in relation to his behaviour in company at the time of their production. In December 1895 Proust and Lucien Daudet were very close and were given, when together, to fits of hysterics. Hearing pretentious or hackneyed sayings (what they called *louchonneries*) would set them off. Proust's eyes, wrote Lucien later, would '[shine] with the diabolical light of uncontrollable laughter';[13] and their behaviour soon caused problems, not least with Robert de Montesquiou, who did not take kindly to being mocked, particularly when he discovered that Proust had a reputation for impersonating his (admittedly peculiar) mannerisms. Marcel's creative self was capable of great things, but what others saw was his outer shell, a curious amalgam of invalid, jester and mother's boy.

His creative self was more than capable of contemplating matters grave and solemn, often intimately tied up with sentiments of guilt. 'Avant la nuit' (Before the night), a short story published in the *Revue blanche* in December 1893 but not included in *Pleasures and Days*, takes the form of a confession by a woman dying from a gunshot self-inflicted because of guilt associated with her lesbianism. 'The Death of Baldassare Sylvande' was published in the *Revue hebdomadaire* in October 1895 and opens *Pleasures and Days* with a tale of a man who has led the indulgent life of a dilettante and tastes authentic experience only in his dying moments. The title character in 'The Confession of a Young Girl' tells her story as she lies dying from a bullet wound inflicted after her mother drops dead upon witnessing her in an adulterous embrace. The collection closes with 'The End of Jealousy', in which the protagonist only manages to overcome his jealous torment after he is fatally injured by a runaway horse in the Bois de Boulogne and realizes he is dying.

Death and the moral and ethical dilemmas that confront us when we reflect on the ways in which we occupy the limited time we have in this life are recurring preoccupations of Proust's early writings. The stark reality of mortality imposed itself on Marcel twice in quick succession in the summer of 1896: Louis Weil, Proust's great uncle and owner of the Auteil house in which he was born, died at the age of 80 in his Paris apartment on 10 May; then Nathé Weil, Louis' brother and Mme Proust's father, died on 30 June. In between these sad events Marcel's book was published, heralded by the pre-publication of Anatole France's brief preface in *Le Figaro* and *Le Gaulois*. Sales, however, were poor. Proust sent out dedicated copies to individuals who might have otherwise bought the book, and due to the format of the work (containing illustrations by Madeleine Lemaire, scores by Reynaldo and Proust's text) its price was almost four times the average cost of a book at the time. Fewer than 350 copies had been sold by 1918 (*Corr.*, XVII, 290) and the initial critical reception was muted. Léon Blum in the *Revue blanche* acknowledged the book's merits but sounded a note of warning: the book was rather *too* polished, *too* pretty; it revealed a talented stylist and a confident, capable mind, but these are gifts, Blum warned, 'that must not be squandered'.[14] Blum was right: the generic range of *Pleasures and Days* is impressive, from the novellas detailing love, loss and psychological tension, to the humorous Flaubertian pastiche 'Bouvard and Pécuchet on Music and Society' and the poetic 'Portraits of Painters and Musicians'. Worldly affairs and society people are depicted with a liberal dose of scepticism or satire; individually the novellas of confession are satisfying; but taken together the whole reads like what it is: the exercises of a subtle and penetrating mind that is still looking for a form that will accommodate its expansiveness.

1896 had been a productive year: by October Proust had filled a good number of loose-leaf sheets and a whole notebook of 110 pages with notes relating to Jean Santeuil. But his health was still problematic. Mme Proust was concerned about her son's consumption of valerian, trional and amyl to help him sleep, and he increasingly relied on a routine of smoking medicated Espic cigarettes and burning Legras and Escouflaire anti-asthmatic powders in order to combat his respiratory 'oppression'. These details may make it all the more surprising to learn that when Jean Lorrain made public insinuations about the nature of Proust's relationship with Lucien Daudet in an article criticizing *Pleasures and Days* in February 1897, Marcel summoned his seconds and challenged Lorrain to a duel with pistols. But such was the practice of the time and honour was at stake. The details of the situation, however, only add to its fascination for twenty-first-century readers. Lorrain was notorious for his acerbic opinions voiced in a weekly column in *Le Journal*. George Painter memorably described him as 'a large, flaccid invert', someone who '[tried] to avert scandal by pretending to be virile and accusing everyone else of perversion.'[15] In his piece in *Le Journal* Lorrain suggests that 'for his next book M. Marcel Proust will get his preface out of M. Alphonse Daudet . . . who will not be able to refuse this preface of his either to Mme Lemaire or to his son Lucien.'[16] This may seem innocuous enough, but Lorrain's position was well known and, as Painter puts it, 'only the most inattentive of *Le Journal*'s hundreds of thousands of readers could fail to understand that this was a public accusation of homosexuality, involving both Proust and Lucien Daudet.'[17] Homosexuality was not illegal but, as William Carter explains, 'social prejudices remained so strong against homosexuality that men feared being branded as such, and hence were subject to blackmail or opprobrium'.[18] The duel was arranged, the men met at the forest of Meudon, and shots were fired. Neither was injured and the business was considered to be over. Reynaldo noted in his journal that Proust's courage, apparently at odds with his nervous temperament, had not in fact surprised him in the slightest. Hahn might have faded somewhat in Proust's affections, but he perhaps recognized better than most that Marcel was not simply a one-trick '*poney*'.

4

# Intellectual, Translator, Mourner

While Proust's personal contretemps with Lorrain flared up and fizzled out, in France a quarrel of far greater proportions, which had been simmering for three years, soon boiled over in spectacular public fashion in January 1898. Alfred Dreyfus, a Jewish army captain on the general staff, was convicted of treason (specifically, selling secrets to the Germans) in late 1894.[1] Anti-Semitic prejudice in France was age-old but had been stirred in the wake of defeat at Sedan and given strident voice in Edouard Drumont's best-selling, scaremongering book *La France juive* (*Jewish France*, 1886) and *La Libre Parole*, the newspaper of the French Anti-Semitic League, first printed in 1892. The prosecution's case rested on a *bordereau*, or memorandum, stolen from a waste-paper basket in the German embassy in Paris, that seemed to show a leak of information from within the French military. Dreyfus was framed as the source of the leak and after his court martial in December 1894 (held behind closed doors in the Cherche-Midi prison) he was publicly degraded at the Ecole Militaire in January 1895, the insignia torn from his uniform and his sabre broken, before a crowd of some 20,000 that gathered at the gates, many of them baying for blood. He was deported the following month to Devil's Island off the coast of French Guiana, where he remained in solitary confinement for most of the next four years, held in a tiny hut in which he was manacled at night and made to eat rotten pork. The debates about the validity of the army's case against him, the scandals, trials, cover-ups and revelations stretched on for many years, dividing the French nation across the social spectrum into Dreyfusards or 'revisionists', who campaigned for a retrial of the man they believed innocent, and anti-Dreyfusards, who believed him guilty and were often establishment figures siding with the army, the government and the Church. Declaring one's position was a perilous business and many relationships were shattered when the ugly uprising of bigotry proved stronger than years-old friendship. Investigative work by Colonel Picquart found the *bordereau* to be a forgery perpetrated by Major Esterhazy but this latter was rapidly acquitted at trial; Picquart was subsequently seconded away from Paris, then suspended from service and finally imprisoned. It was following the injustice of Esterhazy's acquittal that Emile Zola took the step of publishing his open letter 'J'accuse' on 13 January 1898 in *L'Aurore*. Public pressure subsequently led to Dreyfus' return to France for a retrial but he was once again found guilty. He was eventually pardoned in September 1899 and at last rehabilitated in 1906, reinstated in the army, promoted and awarded the Grand-Croix de la Légion d'Honneur, but he was a shadow of the man who had left for Devil's Island ten years before.

Zola had written articles published in *Le Figaro* in November and early December 1897 criticizing Dreyfus' treatment at the hands of the military authorities and calling for truth and justice (Dreyfusard watchwords) but soon anti-Semites, among them Léon Daudet and Maurice Barrès, persuaded the paper to cease circulating such partisan material. Undeterred, Zola published a pamphlet, 'Letter to Youth', which sought the support of students and young people who might follow their conscience in favour of Dreyfus' cause. Proust and his contemporaries sought out signatures for a petition of public support and he and Fernand Gregh triumphed in December 1897, securing Anatole France's signature, a major symbolic achievement given France's status as *Académicien*. With Esterhazy's acquittal in early January, Zola took his biggest risk yet and published 'J'accuse' in *L'Aurore*, which the following day also published the list of signatures gathered by Zola's supporters under the title 'Manifesto of the Intellectuals'. Alongside Anatole France's name were those of Marcel and Robert Proust. This was the birth of intellectual activism as we know it today; indeed the term 'intellectual' dates from this period, although for many anti-Dreyfusards such as Barrès it had a pejorative hue, labelling those it qualified as blinkered, ivory-tower supporters of causes they did not fully understand. And such activism had its risks: Professor Proust, a stalwart of the French establishment and close friend of President Faure, declined to speak to his sons for a week after their names appeared on *L'Aurore*'s front page.

Proust was energized by the Affair. Joseph Reinach, whose seven-volume history of the Affair was published between 1901 and 1911, was closely associated with Mme Straus, whose salon became a Dreyfusard stronghold. Anatole France's support for the cause marked out Mme Arman's salon with the same colours; and up and down France people were gripped by Zola's trial for criminal libel (even Marcel managed to make it to the *cour d'assises* with sandwiches and a flask of coffee to follow proceedings, actions recorded in Jean's name in the notes for *Jean Santeuil*). Throughout *A la recherche* we can watch and listen to the unfolding of the Affair through salon gossip, rumours, betrayals and confrontations, what Proust describes as the shifts in the social kaleidoscope that reconfigure the societal panorama almost overnight, sending individuals' reputations soaring or sinking depending on the predominant prejudice or allegiance in a given milieu. The Affair leaves its mark on the novel not because Proust sought to write a version of *La Débâcle* for his own times but because, given his fascination with the behaviour of individuals in relation to groups, historical events were vitally 'useful', as William Carter notes, 'in discovering the psychological laws that govern human behaviour'.[2] The Affair exposed Proust to the realities of corruption and prejudice; his support for Dreyfus and his eventual incorporation of material relating to the Affair in his mature novel are, most likely, motivated less by a specific sense of Jewish fellow-feeling than by a powerful, principled urge to expose the ugliness and absurdity of bigotry and those who persecute or belittle minorities less powerful than themselves.

The Affair shaped exchanges in cafés, courtrooms and in the columns of newspapers of every stripe. For Proust, however, the conflict of these years was not limited solely to the debates over truth and justice for Alfred Dreyfus. In late 1896 or in 1897 Marcel had a significant argument with his parents. A version of what happened exists in the notes for *Jean Santeuil*: by this account, the confrontation occurred as a result of Mme Proust not purchasing the right colour of gloves (yellow) requested for a rendezvous Marcel had eagerly anticipated with a *demi-mondaine*; in a fit of petulant rage he smashed a glass vase cherished by his mother. An unpublished letter alluded to by Jean-Yves Tadié suggests an alternate source of discord: his parents' discomfort at the impressions created by the photograph taken a few years earlier showing a smug-looking Marcel, seated, with Robert de Flers close behind him and Lucien Daudet by Proust's side, gazing fondly down at him, an arm rested gently upon Proust's shoulder.[3] Was the breakage the result of the temper tantrum of a vain, overgrown child or the poignant, frustrated outburst of a young man unable openly to articulate who he is to the person closest to him in the world? What has survived is a letter from Proust's mother, who casts her own inimitable light on the incident. 'Let's think no more and say no more about it', writes Mme Proust, 'the broken glass will be no more than it is in the temple – the symbol of an indissoluble union' (*Corr.*, II, 161). It is intriguing that Marcel's mother should choose this moment to use an image drawn from the Jewish faith so much under scrutiny – and attack – at the time. In the traditional Jewish wedding ceremony the bride and groom both drink from a glass, which the groom then breaks under his right foot. In making amends with her son, it seems Mme Proust tries to point towards a link of solidarity and love that transcends material things. It is likely that her words, as elsewhere in the correspondence between mother and son, also seek to prepare Marcel for the time when he will have to face a life without her. He quoted them more or less directly in the sketch of the scene he left in *Jean Santeuil* and they feature in Céleste Albaret's remembered account of how Proust had described the scene to her.[4]

Received opinions about Proust cast him as a sedentary soul, a bedridden stranger to daylight. His portraitist Jacques-Emile Blanche described Proust's bedroom as a 'laboratory-sickroom', a hybrid space of experimentation and exhaustion. The years between 1898 and 1904, however, saw a quite different Proust: not exactly a globetrotter like his intrepid father and certainly not an adventurous man of rude health like his tandem-cycling brother, but a traveller nevertheless. In 1898 Marcel made a brief trip to Amsterdam; in 1900 he visited Venice and Padua in April with his mother, Reynaldo and Marie Nordlinger, returning in October that year, alone; 1902 saw his longest ever spell away from his mother – just over two weeks spent with Bertrand de Fénelon in Belgium and Holland; and in 1904 he spent a few days yachting between Cherbourg, Guernsey and Dinard, finding this time, it would seem, better sea legs than had served him on the trip to Belle-Ile-en-Mer with Reynaldo. Amid these major trips were regular late-summer stays in Evian with his mother, dinners in Versailles and, in 1903, Proust's first taste of travelling by motor car, an experience that enthralled him. The dominant force motivating these trips was not sun-worship, however: it was art.

Proust's first, solitary trip to Amsterdam was made to see a major exhibition of paintings by Rembrandt (125 of them); he had written illuminatingly on Chardin and Rembrandt in 1895

Proust with Robert de Flers (left) and Lucien Daudet, with his hand on Proust's shoulder, *c.* 1893.

and wrote another essay, 'Rembrandt', around 1900, stressing once more the importance of the artist's vision over that of the object upon which he gazes, a precept he would develop in *A la recherche*. The trip with Fénelon in 1902 was largely shaped by Proust's desire to see the artistic riches of the Low Countries (above all the 'Flemish Primitives' in Bruges, paintings by Hals in Haarlem, and Vermeer's *View of Delft* in the Mauritshuis in The Hague). The trip about which we know most is Proust's first visit to Venice in April 1900. In this case it was the work of John Ruskin (1819–1900), the English art critic and thinker, and first Slade Professor of Fine Art at Oxford, that lured the young Proust away from the comfort of boulevard Malesherbes. A number of acts of reading, as so often with Proust, lay at the root of his new interest. The *Bulletin de l'Union pour l'action morale*, the journal (to which Proust subscribed) of an organization founded by Paul Desjardins, one of his lecturers at the Ecole Libre des Sciences Politiques, published translated extracts from Ruskin's writings between 1893 and 1903. And between December 1895 and March 1897 *La Revue des deux mondes* published excerpts of a study of Ruskin by Robert de La Sizeranne, entitled *Ruskin et la religion de la beauté* (*Ruskin and the Religion of Beauty*). From these pages there emanated the voice of a writer who spoke directly to the Proust of the hawthorn paths and sun-dappled fields, a critical thinker who looked on the world with fresh eyes, who saw beauty in the simplest and most mundane of things, who appreciated architecture, painting and the plastic arts like no other.

One wonders whether Proust paused to peruse the article preceding the pages on Ruskin in the *Revue des deux mondes* for March 1897; if he did he would have seen mention, in an extraordinarily dry article on the fabrication of matches in France (part of a series on 'Insalubrious Industries'), of the important work in the field of public hygiene of one Professor Proust. Most likely he swept eagerly past these pages to those of La Sizeranne, which struck within him a long, resonant chord. The magic of Ruskin's words took a lasting grip on Proust; the translation and annotating of two of the English master's works would become Proust's major intellectual undertaking of the next eight years.

Proust was introduced in 1896 to Marie Nordlinger, Reynaldo's highly cultured English cousin who had left Manchester College of Art to pursue her studies and training in Paris. In December 1899 he told her in a letter that for a fortnight he had been occupied with 'a little bit of work absolutely different to what I generally do, relating to Ruskin and certain cathedrals' (*Corr.*, II, 377). Ruskin died just over six weeks later and the breadth of reference and sensitive, knowledgeable discussion that shapes the obituary notice by Proust published in *La Chronique des arts et de la curiosité* gives a sense of just how intensely he had already got to grips with the Englishman's writings. Proust's second published essay, 'Pelerinages ruskiniens en France' ('Ruskinian Pilgrimages in France'), which appeared in *Le Figaro* on 13 February 1900, has a similar, reverential tone, but while its author seeks to sing the praises of the recently departed, the piece also provides a glimpse of the aesthetic considerations that will be explored at greater length in *Time Regained*. Ruskin was a normal mortal like the rest of us, Proust writes, but he managed to set forth precious ideas from his 'perishable mind' in his books, thus giving them '*une demeure non pas éternelle, sans doute, mais dont la durée sera du moins plus en rapport avec les services qu'elles pourront rendre à l'humanité*' (not, doubtless, an eternal residence, but one whose duration will be at least more in keeping with the services that they will be able to render to humanity; *CSB*, 443). Here, with characteristic humility and lightness of touch, in coming to terms with the death of a master, Proust articulates not a religious faith, which was the backbone of Ruskin's work, but faith in the enduring power of the written word.

Proust's sensitivity to the finitude of human existence was not provoked by Ruskin's death alone. Eighteen months earlier his mother had undergone a risky operation for a uterine fibroma

Proust contemplative in Venice, May 1900.

that left her, for a time, in an extremely precarious state. It was a sobering reminder to her son that their cherished time together was not without limit. After three months of convalescence, however, Mme Proust was returned to good health and playing once more her vital part in her son's new intellectual venture. Marcel's English was scant at best; his initial acquaintance with Ruskin was through the translated extracts he had pored over in the *Bulletin de l'Union pour l'action morale* and through La Sizeranne's study. His mother's English, however, was very solid. Proust's 'translation' of Ruskin, then, was a challenge to which he rose in characteristically idiosyncratic fashion. His regime of working late at night and sleeping through the morning (and sometimes the early afternoon) was one of which his mother did not approve, but which she tolerated since Marcel appeared at last to have latched on to a worthy project with lasting enthusiasm. Their modus operandi was a curious one, but one that yielded impressive results: Mme Proust, upon rising, would find notes from her son requesting her renderings of this or that section of *The Bible of Amiens*, Ruskin's study of the statuary (in particular of the portals of the west facade) of Amiens Cathedral. Mme Proust would oblige and when his day began several hours later, with Ruskin's original before him, and Mme Proust's word-for-word crib in hand, Marcel would apply himself to rendering French (and, one might argue, to 'Proustifying') Ruskin's text. When he had a draft he was happy with he would check dictionaries and other sources, and contact friends and acquaintances in pursuit of details, definitions, the *mot juste*. Marie Nordlinger, a native English speaker also fluent in French, was a major help to Marcel. Her assistance was even greater in Proust's second Ruskin translation, that of *Sesame and Lilies*, Ruskin's lectures on reading and the education of women published in 1865, for which she provided much of the initial crib.

Proust's trip to Venice in 1900 was driven by a desire to see for himself the buildings and the artworks about which Ruskin had written. But as was often the case for Proust, first-hand experience needed to be mediated: his trip to Belgium and Holland was seen through the lens of pages of Taine and Fromentin read as he walked from gallery to gallery; in Venice, Ruskin was his guide: Marie read to Proust from *The Stones of Venice* as they sheltered from a storm in St Mark's Basilica, leaving him 'strangely moved and seemingly uplifted in ecstasy' by the experience.[5] Proust's letters to Marie reveal his courteous and flattering side; they show how relentlessly demanding and focused he could be when his mind was occupied by a specific goal; they reveal his wit and sense of humour; and reports on his health are not infrequent. 'I'm in an atrocious state . . . trembling with fever and choking with asthma', he writes in August 1903. In October that year he ruefully chronicles his pilgrimages to Normandy and Burgundy:

I've dragged across France, from Roman vestibules to Gothic chevets, an ardent curiosity and a body that is more and more unwell. And of the monuments I've visited only the Hospices of Beaune were suited to my acute state of illness. I don't doubt that I would have been admitted as an emergency case. Viollet-le-Duc said that the Hospices were so beautiful that they made you want to fall ill in Beaune. It's clear that he didn't know what it was to be ill. (*Corr.*, III, 427)

At once witty, learned and grave, these comments bear witness to the constant tension between Proust's perishable body and the stamina and resilience of his mind. One suspects a degree of poetic licence (with regard to his suffering) in letters such as this, but Marie's own account of her companion's state tallies with Proust's. She wrote of Proust's '*esprit sans cesse en éveil*' (ceaselessly alert mind), which 'didn't give in to the illness which hounded his body'.[6]

Despite his fragility, when he visited Venice with his mother he did not travel light. His travelling companions were multiple volumes of Ruskin: *Saint Mark's Rest*, *Modern Painters*, *The Bible of Amiens* and, of course, *The Stones of Venice*. During this period Proust also read Emile Mâle's *The Religious Art of the Thirteenth Century in France*, a work which, along with Ruskin, informs the depiction of one of the most memorable sites of *A la recherche*, the Combray church. In the novel the narrator describes the church as

entirely different from the rest of the town: an edifice occupying, so to speak, a four-dimensional space – the name of the fourth being Time – extending through the centuries its ancient nave, which, bay after bay, chapel after chapel, seemed to stretch across and conquer not merely a few yards of soil, but each successive epoch from which it emerged triumphant. (*Swann's Way*, 71; I, 60)

The study of Ruskin (and Mâle, with whom Proust would later correspond) was at the root of this fascination with duration through time, a central concern of the mature novel.

Although he constantly complained of his health problems, between 1899 and the end of 1902 Proust managed better than ever to travel, to entertain and to work. A favourite haunt of the time was the café-restaurant Weber on the rue Royale where Proust, wrapped up in his woollens under his coat like a fragile curio, would appear around half-past-seven in the evening, nibbling the edges of his moustache and sipping a glass of grappa, and declare 'that he had just got up, that he had the flu, that he was going to go back to bed, that the noise was making him ill', and would then remain for hours, proffering 'remarks of an extraordinary novelty and devilishly perceptive insights, in a tone at once hesitant and hasty', fascinating his companions with his ability to pursue several lines of thought at once.[7] And this capacity to think plurally noted by Daudet can be observed in Proust's working patterns and in the textures of his writing. While still completing *Pleasures and Days* he was drafting scenes relating to Jean Santeuil; and now, with the Jean Santeuil notes all but abandoned by the end of 1899, and work well under way on his translation of *The Bible of Amiens*, between 1903 and 1904 Proust produced a series of five pieces for *Le Figaro*, published under the heading 'Salons parisiens', chronicling the character, atmosphere and the dramatis personae of the much talked about salons of the Princesse Mathilde, Madeleine Lemaire, the Princesse de Polignac, the Comtesse d'Haussonville and the Comtesse Potocka. The first two of these pieces were signed 'Dominique', the others 'Horatio'; thus briefly (for he was soon enough identified) Proust revelled in listening to the socialites talking unguardedly about his writing, unaware that he was the author of whom they spoke. His talent for mimicry, his wit and eye for detail shine through in these pieces, which in their reproduction of traits of character and tics of language anticipate his brilliant pastiches of Flaubert, Balzac, the Goncourts and others published in *Le Figaro* just a few years later.

As we survey these years of Proust's life it is interesting to contrast his personal trajectory with that of the age in which he lived. In 1900 France was feting the coming of a new age, the opening of the Paris Metro and another, even grander World's Fair. Freud published *The Interpretation of Dreams*, Max Planck formulated his theory of the quantum and Picasso first came to Paris: Paris, as Gertrude Stein stated, 'was where the twentieth century was'.[8] But in the early years of the new century Proust, in mind and often in body, was elsewhere. When the Metro opened he was hundreds of miles away in Venice, on the trail of ancient art and architecture. Thanks to *A la recherche du temps perdu*, Proust's place in the pantheon of modernism is firmly cemented; but as the new century broke, his gaze was resolutely fixed on the past. This is not to say that he was uninterested in the developments of his day, simply that in forging his own aesthetic, coming to his own views on the world and the beauty it contains, he first wanted to acquaint himself with those who had come before him, with Rembrandt, Vermeer and Hals, and with the artistic heritage of Ruskin and the artists he admired: Carpaccio, Bellini, Giotto, Tiepolo. Proust had largely left behind the briefer forms (sketches, short stories, novellas) of *Pleasures and Days* as he tried to develop *Jean Santeuil*, but this had come to an impasse. Or rather, it had yielded an accumulation of disparate fragments; some of the ingredients were in place, but the pieces would not splice and cohere into a whole; to use Roland Barthes' mayonnaise metaphor, the novel would not *take*.[9] As William Carter justly notes, 'the absent elements' in Proust's first attempt at a novel 'were the vital organs of fiction: plot, point of view, and structure'.[10] These notes were a vital stepping stone towards the writing of *A la recherche* and a good many fragments form the basis for episodes in the finished work; but to call *Jean Santeuil* a novel, even an unfinished one, is to overstate the case. Its published state is the posthumous result of the sorting and sifting of editors, who grouped fragments thematically and by the apparent age of the protagonist. What Proust abandoned around 1899 in favour of the new challenge of translation and annotation was an unsuccessful search for a voice. Translation afforded him the opportunity of trying out the voice of another; the process would continue with the pastiches of 1908.

It had been a busy year and 1900 ended in upheaval for the family: Professor and Mme Proust decided to leave their home of almost 30 years on the boulevard Malesherbes for a larger apartment at 45 rue de Courcelles, near the Parc Monceau. The move was made during Proust's trip to Venice in October. A downturn in his health in the new year brought with it a veil of gloom. On 31 January he wrote to his friend Constantin de Brancovan, the brother of Anna de Noailles and editor of *La Renaissance latine*, complaining of having suffered from flu since New Year's Day. The portrait Proust paints is stark: 'always ill, without pleasures, without a goal, without action, without ambition, with my life finished before me, and the sense of the sorrow that I'm causing my parents, I have very little joy' (*Corr.*, II, 416). The one comfort he does have, he remarks, is the solace of his friendships. And while Proust remained in regular contact with Lucien and Reynaldo, new favourites were now attracting his attentions. He met Prince Antoine Bibesco (1878–1951) and his brother Emmanuel (1877–1917) in June 1899. The family, who belonged to the Romanian nobility and were related to the Brancovans, lived on the rue de Courcelles, close to the Prousts' new apartment. Proust and Antoine, a young diplomat, were soon close, confiding in each other and developing a private coded language they used between themselves and with Vicomte Bertrand de Fénelon (1878–1914), a handsome, blue-eyed Frenchman of ancient noble blood who took up his first diplomatic posting in Constantinople in December 1902, to the besotted Marcel's great chagrin. In the friends' letters, information that must not be further divulged is marked *tombeau* (to be taken to the grave); they refer to each other in reversed oranagrammatized forms: Marcel is 'Lecram', Bibesco 'Ocsebib' and Fénelon 'Nonelef'. A recurring topic of discussion between Marcel and Antoine is who may or may not be *salaïste*, a term of their own invention meaning homosexual (calqued on the name of Antoine de Sala, a diplomat whose preference for those of his own sex was well known). Bibesco, who it seems enjoyed such discussions but was attracted only to women, had aspirations as a playwright, while his brother Emmanuel was extremely knowledgeable in the domain of architecture, possessing a significant collection of photographs of Gothic churches. In 1902 or 1903 the friends travelled together to visit a number of churches and cathedrals within driving distance of Paris, daytime fieldwork to complement the task of translation that occupied Proust's nights.

Proust's thirtieth year had started with a month-long flu and his nocturnal working regime took its toll on his fragile frame: going to bed sometimes at midday (or later) and rising in the late evening meant that often he would have only one meal per day. When his parents took a break in Zermatt in Switzerland in August 1901 his mother left with the hope that she would return to find that he had gained weight, evidence of an improved regime. This provoked some entertaining letters from Proust to his mother, recalling the gargantuan appetite of his youth ('two tournedos steaks of which I didn't leave a scrap, a whole plate of fried potatoes, cream cheese, Gruyère, two croissants'; *Corr.*, II, 444), but the effects on his waistline were negligible and his health worries persisted, fuelled by his reading about the treatment of asthma. Did he, Proust wondered, have worms that were causing his attacks? Should he have a mercury enema? Such were the preoccupations that jostled with thoughts of Ruskin and the architecture of medieval churches.

In Proust's letters to Antoine Bibesco in 1901 we find poems, flattery and flirtation. This continues in 1902 but gradually Proust's attentions turn increasingly towards Fénelon. Proust's interest quickly became tinged with jealousy stirred by thoughts of Bertrand's unknown activities during Marcel's illness-induced absences. 'I envy you, Nonelef and you,' he writes to Bibesco, 'I envy each of you seeing the other while all the distraction I've got is turning over in bed' (*Corr.*, III, 62). He asked Bibesco to spy on Fénelon, to inform him of how Bertrand spent his time and with whom. Bertrand may have had a mistress when Proust first met him (a remark in a notebook from 1908 suggests Proust believed this to be the case); a mutual acquaintance, Paul Morand, wrote later that Fénelon was bisexual; but since much of their correspondence was destroyed and what remains is almost exclusively undisclosed, in private hands, it is impossible to determine with any certainty the nature of their relationship. What is clear is that Proust was enormously fond of Fénelon and that the trip to Belgium and Holland with him later in 1902 was a tortured affair on a personal, emotional level for Proust, most likely since he was unsure of Fénelon's preferences and fearful of destroying a friendship he cherished. He was tasting independence for the first time, keeping largely regular hours, his asthma was in abeyance, he was viewing works of art and sights that nourished the deepest fibres of his sensibility and yet, as he put it in a sorrowful letter to his mother from Amsterdam, he was 'in such a disastrous sentimental state that I feared poisoning poor Fénelon's trip with my sadness' (*Corr.*, III, 163). Happiness, it seemed, could not come from company.[11]

Yet isolation, in this period, was also a source of unhappiness for Proust, who repeatedly complained about his solitary existence and the physical and mental suffering provoked by his illness. When the time came for Bertrand to leave for Constantinople in December

1902, Proust snapped at an ill-judged remark and set about his friend with his fists before trampling and tearing to pieces Fénelon's brand new top hat. This untrammelled rage (the frustration that his health would never permit him the freedom – or the sustained company – of those he most desired?) echoes his breaking his mother's vase five years earlier. In *The Guermantes Way* a stern dressing down from Charlus provokes in the narrator a similar rage that sees him lay waste to the baron's top hat. In the novel the narrator attributes this reaction to his frustration at the pride and bombast of the haughty aristocrat (in which Charlus shares much with Montesquiou); Proust's reflection on the actual event offers some insight into how fraught matters could be between mother and son. Enclosing a piece of Fénelon's hat brim as proof of what happened, forced by the hours he keeps to write rather than speak to his mother living under the same roof, he blames her for the nervous state that caused him to explode at Fénelon's remark. 'The truth', he claims, 'is that as soon as I'm doing well, the life that makes me do well exasperates you and you demolish everything, up to the point that I'm ill again.' He feels that she is only kindly and tolerant towards him when he is ill: 'it's sad not to be able to have at once affection and health' (*Corr.*, III, 191). These cutting words encapsulate the central dilemma of Proust's life in the years before his parents' deaths. His illness made him suffer greatly and his mother's love provided emotional succour; yet as soon as she tried – with the best possible intentions – to extract him from his nocturnal routine (by refusing to allow the servants to make him meals or answer his calls at odd hours), he felt that his health suffered for it. And although Ruskin's spark provided the light and the energy that saw him through his lucubrations, his enthusiasm was waning. 'All I'm doing isn't real work' ('*n'est pas du vrai travail*'), he wrote to Bibesco a fortnight after Fénelon's departure. Ideas, profiles of characters for novels, he said, were gathering in his mind, but without substance: they seemed merely to underscore for him the emptiness of his existence (*Corr.*, III, 196).

By marked contrast, Marcel's brother Robert, a promising medical career under way, was rapidly fulfilling the hopes of his parents. He was to be married early in 1903 to Marthe Dubois-Amiot but Mme Proust, who had painful rheumatism, was additionally suffering from the early stages of kidney disease and was unable to attend the civil ceremony on 31 January. Marcel was also absent; he had not slept for three nights. His mother was brought to the church ceremony on 2 February in an ambulance but was not strong enough to attend the reception and luncheon afterwards. Proust made it to the church, and managed to perform his role as best man to his younger brother. Pallid and drawn, and fearful of catching a chill, he padded out his suit with thermogene wadding, a sort of medicated cotton wool, and wore – it is said – three coats and a swathe of assorted woollens. Valentine Thomson, Proust's eighteen-year-old cousin, was accompanied by this bizarre-looking figure as she took around the collection plate: all Marcel could do was apologize for the appearance and unwieldy bulk of his insulated form that prevented him from following his cousin along the aisles.[12] Photographic evidence of this occasion, alas, has not survived.

It may have taken Proust a fortnight to recover from the wedding but he soon had reason for cheer: extracts from his translation of *The Bible of Amiens* appeared in *La Renaissance latine* and they were positively received. His first two 'Salon' pieces were published in *Le Figaro* in late February and early May but with the second of these came the seasonal intensification of his illness – hay fever, asthma, fevers and bronchitis kept Proust in bed until June: the cycle seemed unbreakable. By August, however, Proust was able to leave Paris for Evian. He took an overnight train to Avallon from which he saw the sunrise, an event of natural beauty that would be inscribed memorably, in due course, together with the drama of sunset, in his novel. While in Evian at the Splendide Hôtel with his parents, whom he joined there, Proust was visited by Louis d'Albufera, another aristocratic acquaintance (he was the great-grandson of a Maréchal d'Empire) he had met through either Bibesco or Fénelon, and his mistress, the actress Louisa de Mornand. With this couple Proust forged another trio of the sort he had formed with Gaston de Caillavet and Jeanne Pouquet. He was an intimate of Louis and his mistress and an intermediary for the pair, helping to pass letters and patch up the (frequent) quarrels between the fiery Louisa and the dim but charming 'Albu'. The couple's passionate relationship lent much to Proust's lovers Saint-Loup and Rachel (a jealous aristocrat and an actress); equally, traits of Louisa are to be found in Odette Swann, a character who additionally owes much to Laure Hayman, the *demi-mondaine* mistress of Proust's Uncle Louis. Although George Painter and some of Proust's early commentators would have us believe otherwise, the characters (and indeed the places) of *A la recherche* are almost never drawn from a single biographical source: they are composite, alloying memory, observation and invention.

In late July 1903 Professor Proust was invited back to Illiers, a celebrated son of the town, in order to officiate at the school prize-giving. The previous month he had inaugurated a monument to Pasteur in Chartres. Such activities (not to mention the countless meetings and the international summits of recent years) took time and sapped energy, and Adrien was almost 70. Late in 1903 the end came suddenly. On 24 November, at the Faculty of Medicine, preparing to preside over a thesis defence and feeling unwell, Professor Proust retired to the lavatory but did not reappear. Robert, who had been concerned by Adrien's appearance earlier in the day, forced the door on the cubicle and found his father unconscious; he had suffered a stroke. He was taken home to the rue de Courcelles, where he died on the morning of 26 November. On the intervening day while Adrien lingered in death's antechamber, Robert's wife Marthe gave birth to a baby girl, Adrienne Suzanne (later known as Suzy). In his responses to letters of condolence Proust explained his sense of gratitude that his illness, forcing him to spend a great deal of

Mme Proust and her
sons, *c.* 1896.

time at home, had permitted him a closer proximity to his father
than a healthy existence would have granted. He feared deeply for
his mother who, despite an outer showing of fortitude, was surely
suffering unspeakably at the loss of the man to whom she had
devoted 'every minute of her life' (*Corr.*, III, 446). Life had to start
afresh, Proust recognized, but his lack of drive and direction was
overwhelming. He was dissuaded from abandoning the almost
finished work on *The Bible of Amiens* by his mother, however, who
explained that Adrien's abiding wish had been to see the project
come to fruition. So Proust returned to his proofs and finally on 22
February 1904 *The Bible of Amiens*, prefaced and heavily annotated,
was published by the Mercure de France, bearing the dedication 'To
the memory of my father, struck down at his workplace on November

24, 1903.' With Robert and Marthe now in a family home of their own, in the rue de Courcelles, *petit Marcel* was now the man of the house. He and his mother formed a curious couple: she somewhat corpulent, weary, bereft; and he sallow, slight and searching, still, for a voice and a form that might make his beloved mother proud.

Jeanne had rallied for the sake of her family when her husband died, but as her state at Robert's wedding had already suggested, she had significant health problems of her own. Ever conscious of Marcel's fragility and unwilling to add to his suffering, however, she kept her mental and physical travails largely to herself. By September 1904 she felt able to take her first holiday alone, travelling to Dieppe, from where she wrote of bracing walks, buffeted by the chill winds from the Channel. Around the same time Marcel was engaged in the translation of Ruskin's *Sesame and Lilies* but these labours were providing scant rewards. Of Ruskin, already in January 1904, he had grumbled to Marie Nordlinger that 'this old man is starting to annoy me' (*Corr.*, IV, 49). He would soon, however, be engaged in the composition of the introductory essay to the work, 'On Reading', a creative, reflective meditation on a simple yet profound, enchanting and illuminating pleasure (above all of childhood). *This* was real work, an essay that throngs with anticipations of the mature novel, and whose production, in the depths of night, under harsh electric light early in 1905, cost Marcel significant pain in his eyes. Indeed, in September 1904, drifting from the business of translation, he was greatly preoccupied by his health, writing a letter to an ex-colleague of his father specializing in gastric medicine. It became so detailed and lengthy that in the end Proust did not send it: it was found among the papers in his apartment at his death eighteen years later.

The letter seeks a second opinion on whether, as recommended to him by Dr Brissaud, an asthma specialist, he should undergo psychotherapeutic treatment in the clinic of Dr Sollier, a neurologist who had treated Anna de Noailles for nervous (we would now probably say post-natal) depression in 1901. Such treatment, Proust feared (isolation, immobilization, *suralimentation* or increased feeding) may do more harm than good. 'I am, it seems', he notes, '(from a medical perspective), lots of different things, although in truth no one has ever really known what' (*Corr.*, IV, 250). This rather neatly captures his enigmatic status but for good measure the letter's twelve pages then go on to detail his asthma, arthritic symptoms, the results of urine analysis, his bowel movements, gastric health (he must stand, or at least lie, on a chaise longue for as many as eight hours after eating a meal). Proust – and his parents – may have feared that he was lacking in will, but this letter reveals it in spades: a powerful will to observe, record, analyse, classify and to seek to understand. That this letter was not sent is revealing of the therapeutic function of writing for Proust. Having worked through his symptoms and asked his various questions (just as he outlined his interests and posed endless questions to Charles Grandjean about his possible career path in 1893), Proust is able to come to his own conclusions. He did, in the end, stay for a spell in Dr Sollier's sanatorium from early December 1905 to 25 January 1906, although the medical benefits of the 'treatment' seem to have been few: Proust mainly went in order to satisfy his filial conscience in fulfilling a promise he had made to his mother, who had been eager that he at least take consultation on his condition.

To Robert Dreyfus in May 1905 Proust explained that he was leading 'a very quiet, restful life of reading and very studious intimacy with Maman' (*Corr.*, V, 147). The following month, after burning a great deal of midnight oil and suffering some exceptionally extended bouts of asthma (attacks over ten successive days, according to one letter, and, just a few days later, a single attack lasting over 30 hours; *Corr.*, V, 189; 200), 'On Reading' was published in *La Renaissance latine*. The essay was an introduction to *Sesame and Lilies* but more importantly it represented an emancipation of his own thinking from that of the writer in whose service he had laboured for almost a decade. Against Ruskin's claims that reading amounts to the passive absorption of the words of the great minds of the past, Proust argues that reading brings us to the threshold of the life of the mind, incites us to think for ourselves but does not in itself constitute that *vie spirituelle*. With these balanced, forceful yet elegant pages, the voice that we know now as 'Proustian' made itself heard.

Proust travelled to Evian in September with his mother but almost as soon as they arrived she was taken ill. Her kidneys were failing and her body slowly shutting down. Robert rushed to the resort and escorted his stoical, reluctant mother home: she had wanted to be photographed by Mme Catusse in order to leave a memento for Marcel, although she was anxious her suffering would mar the image left for posterity. When Proust returned home a few days later (his mother had requested that he stay on in Evian, an attempt to spare him the spectacle of her final hours), Mme Proust was still alive but she had deteriorated and was refusing food and medication. She died on 26 September 1905. Marcel now was alone: his father was gone and with his mother's passing he was abruptly cut loose from the last remaining ballast of his fragile existence. In 1942 when Marie Nordlinger published her letters from Marcel she omitted those he wrote to her upon his mother's death, deeming their publication indelicate since 'in them he revealed his wound with such complete abandon'.[13] Proust was troubled by the suffering caused for his mother in her final days by her concerns about his ability to survive alone after her death. He described his mother's life as 'an uninterrupted sacrifice' (*Corr.*, v, 341) and articulated, to Mme de Noailles, his conception of the scale of his loss: 'She takes my life with her, like father had taken hers' (*Corr.*, v, 345). Proust's mother – his collaborator, companion and conscience – was gone, and with her ended the life of *petit Marcel*.

# 5

# Beginnings and Endings

I will be more and more ill, I will miss those I have lost more and
more, all that I had managed to dream of life will be more and
more inaccessible.
Letter to Mme Straus, July 1906

These words are eloquent of Proust's mental state in the months
following his mother's death. They were prompted by the declaration
of Alfred Dreyfus' innocence and his reinstatement (and that of
Picquart) in the army. Dreyfus and Picquart had seen their suffering
and disappointment become joy and 'delicious triumph'. But this
turnaround for Proust underscores what he saw as the hopelessness
of his own situation. While Dreyfus' and Picquart's torment was
founded on errors, injustices for which reparation was possible,
the suffering Proust was experiencing rested upon 'physiological
truths, human and sentimental truths' (*Corr.*, VI, 159). As the world
looked to Proust at this time, there was no succour, merely aching
isolation and a struggle for breath.

In late January 1906 Proust had returned to the rue de Courcelles
from Dr Sollier's sanatorium, but the apartment was too large and
too expensive; full of memories, it was a 'real and dear cemetery'
(*Corr.*, VI, 312). He needed to find somewhere more suited to his
needs but, as he explained to his old friend Jeanne Pouquet, now
Mme Gaston de Caillavet, he did not have the courage to take a

place with which his mother had not been familiar. He was unable to keep the hours necessary to visit potential properties, so obliging friends made numerous viewings on his behalf. For Marcel there was only really ever one contender: the apartment at 102 boulevard Haussmann that had been his great-uncle Louis Weil's Paris residence. The comforting knowledge that his mother had often dined here was enough to make him overlook the noise and dust of the busy boulevard, along with the pollen of its trees that so threatened his respiratory health, and make this rather unsuitable address home for the next thirteen years.

He did not move in until December 1906; the early part of that year was spent adjusting to life alone, gradually starting to accept visits from friends again in February and completing his work on the second Ruskin translation: *Sésame et les lys* finally appeared in June. Although it was positively reviewed, the publication did not bring joy. Robert's career blossomed as his father's had before him and he travelled to the United States and then to a major conference of French-language doctors in Canada. While those close to him spread their wings, even Marcel's dreams of life, as he put it to Mme Straus, seemed 'more and more inaccessible'. A rare source of solace was found in railway timetables, which Proust devoured, cooking up 'a thousand circular tours' while lying on his chaise longue between two and six in the morning (*Corr.*, vi, 167). In 'Swann in Love' he would describe such documents as 'the most intoxicating romance in the lover's library' (*Swann's Way*, 352; i, 288) and the narrator would later pore wistfully over timetables and advertisements for such tours, imagining trips to 'Balbec' (Cabourg) and further afield, to Florence, Venice and Pisa, prompted by the magic of the names listed before him (*Swann's Way*, 464–73; i, 378–86).

Proust felt able to plan a trip away from Paris in August but this was fraught with difficulties. Was there somewhere in Trouville or nearby that was 'good and dry, *not in the trees*, elevated but not over the valley where there is fog (elevated, I mean not in the town, but on the beach suits me fine), with electricity if possible, of new-ish construction, neither dusty . . . nor humid . . .'? (*Corr.*, VI, 168). Unsurprisingly, these criteria were not easily fulfilled; instead Marcel made a sudden decision, opting for the familiar surroundings of the Hôtel des Réservoirs at Versailles, where he was to stay for almost five months until his definitive move to 102 boulevard Haussmann on 27 December. With a likely nod to Flaubert's famous reclusiveness at Croisset, he referred to himself in a letter to Reynaldo as 'the hermit of Versailles' (*Corr.*, VI, 316), but his lengthy seclusion did not happen by design. Rather, wrangling with his brother over their parents' furniture and protracted indecisiveness about the decor of the apartment on boulevard Haussmann prolonged the stay. Marcel addressed countless letters to Mme Catusse about how the apartment should look, in one of which he refers to the re-homing of the rue de Courcelles furniture in his new apartment as the recreation of '*la patrie perdue*' (the lost homeland; *Corr.*, VI, 302). It would be several years until Proust would formulate his now celebrated axiom that 'the true paradises are the paradises that we have lost' (*Time Regained*, 222; IV, 449), but his observation regarding the furniture suggests that the sentiments upon which it was founded were felt already in 1906.

Aside from his letters, Proust's pen had been idle since the completion of *Sésame et les lys*. But this soon changed with a most peculiar turn of events. On 24 January 1907 Henri van Blarenberghe, the son of a family known to the Prousts, killed his mother and then took his own life. Gaston Calmette, *Le Figaro*'s director, knew that Proust had been acquainted with Van Blarenberghe and invited him to write a comment piece for the paper. Grieving his own mother and still coming to terms with his own sense of guilt at the suffering he caused her, Proust accepted this commission: life seemed to have played out a scenario akin to those he had imagined in 'Before Night' (1893) and, in particular, 'A Young Girl's Confession' (1896). In a burst of creative energy Proust wrote the piece between 3 a.m. and 8 a.m.; he stopped only because of the pain in his hand (he was, after all, 'out of the habit of writing'; *Corr.*, VII, 62). The resulting article, 'Sentiments filiaux d'un parricide' (Filial Sentiments of a Parricide) is a fascinating moment in Proust's trajectory: its themes – memory, our connection to the past, child-parent relations, guilt, expiation – are those of *A la recherche*; they were also issues lodged, unshifting in his mind at least since the death of his mother the previous September. A contingent event provided Proust the opportunity to recommence his search for a voice and, con-comitantly, to confront and move beyond issues by which he had risked being overwhelmed.

Marcel's pen was now back firmly in his hand and, although he complained increasingly of hand and eye pain in the years to come, hereafter it seldom rested during his waking hours. 1907 saw three further significant publications, all of them containing elements that work their way (sometimes verbatim) into *A la recherche du temps perdu*. There was a piece (supposed to be a review) prompted by the memoirs of Mme de Boigne (1781–1866) in March; a celebration of Anna de Noailles' poetry in June; and an essay recounting the exhilaration of motor car travel in November. The generic fluidity is revealing of Proust's creative drive in this period. Neither the piece on Mme de Boigne's memoirs nor that on Noailles' *Les Eblouissements* (*Resplendence*) is, strictly speaking, a review. In the former, entitled 'Journées de lecture' ('Days of Reading') Proust takes his lead from Mme de Boigne's book (it is seen as a means of accessing the past) but much of the first half of his article treats the telephone and how it has become the preferred contemporary means of connecting disparate places. In this Proust revisits a scene based on a phone call to his mother that was written into the *Jean Santeuil* notes in 1896 and anticipates an important scene of recognition (*The Guermantes Way*, 146–51; II, 431–5) in which the narrator's telephone call to his grandmother painfully reveals, through the isolated timbres of her voice, the extent of the deterioration in her health, which habit had masked from his view in their day-to-day dealings. In the second half of 'Days of Reading' Proust holds forth on the magic of proper names, particularly those of the nobility, whose iteration in the present conjures up links to people, places and their historical past. Here Proust is anticipating what will become a central preoccupation of the narrator in *A la recherche*, namely the associative power that names have to shuttle he or she who contemplates them back and forth in time and place – a preoccupation that was already present in Proust's comments about railway timetables quoted above.

The review essay on Anna de Noailles' *Les Eblouissements* is of a quite different tone but is every bit as revealing of its author's developing sensibility. A reader of Proust's correspondence is struck by the strong, spiritual rapport between Noailles and Proust: their sensibilities (defined by their nerves and aesthetic refinement) were very much attuned, and this fellow feeling suffuses Proust's essay of June 1907. A striking feature is the celebration in Noailles' poetry of what readers of *Against Sainte-Beuve* and *A la recherche* will recognize as one of the foundations of Proust's mature thinking: 'all that can constitute the contingent, social self of Mme de Noailles . . . is not spoken of once in the course of these four-hundred pages', writes Proust: instead, what dominates is 'the deep self [*le moi profond*] that individualizes works and makes them last' (*csb*, 536–7). In the poet's methods we find an affinity with Proust's aesthetic in *A la recherche*: he praises the metaphors found in Noailles' work that 'substitute for the observation of that which is, the resurrection of what we have felt (the only truly interesting reality)' (*csb*, 542). Sensation has a privileged place in *A la recherche*, as the madeleine scene in *Swann's Way* famously illustrates. Although undoubtedly genuine in its praise of Noailles, between the lines of this critical essay a reader of *A la recherche* may perceive the formulation of a sort of mission statement, a precursor to *Against Sainte-Beuve*, a follow-up or pendant to 'Against Obscurity'.

Although he had been productive in the early months of the year, Proust was at the same time driven to distraction by the 'martyrdom' imposed on him (*Corr.*, VII, 103) by the noise of workmen making modifications to neighbouring properties during the (daytime) hours when he would normally sleep. Predictably his health suffered: 'I have wiped my nose eighty-three times while writing this letter', he remarked to Hahn in February (*Corr.*, VII, 72). He had kept in his service a valet and Félicie Fiteau, his parents' cook and household servant. In February he re-hired Nicolas Cottin, who had previously served his parents but had been dismissed because of a tendency to drink, and in May Cottin's wife Céline joined the household to assist the elderly Félicie. Despite this domestic help, when it came to organizing a dinner to honour Gaston Calmette, the director of *Le Figaro* who had published much of Proust's recent writing, he decided to rent a private dining room at the Ritz rather than entertain at home as he had done during his parents' lifetime. From this point onward Proust increasingly frequented and hosted guests at the temple to luxury created by Auguste Escoffier and César Ritz on the Place Vendôme. The apartment at 102 boulevard Haussmann was to be a sanctuary away from the champagne and chandeliers, providing the solitude he required for writing. The dinner for Calmette took place on 1 July and was attended by a select group, among whom were Anna de Noailles, Jacques-Emile Blanche, Louis d'Albufera and Emmanuel Bibesco (neither Mme Straus nor Mme Arman de Caillavet was able to attend, much to Proust's sadness). The after-dinner recital included music by Fauré, Beethoven, Chopin and Wagner. The evening was a great success, about which Proust wrote enthusiastically to Hahn, who was in London.

Proust and Hahn's correspondence is particularly interesting in the years following the death of Mme Proust, for in it we find Proust expressing the childish side of his character that had been sustained (one might say hypertrophied) by his overbearing mother. Proust and Hahn's private language is still enthusiastically, insistently used by Proust well into his thirties. He normally signs himself off 'Buncht' or 'Gruncht', while Hahn is addressed variously as 'Buninuls', 'Binchnibuls' or 'Hibuls' among many others, whose derivation is unclear. French spellings are altered: *souffrant* (ill, uncomfortable) becomes '*sousfrant*'; *tendresse* (tenderness), '*tendresche*'; *couché* (lying down), '*kousché*'; *Adieu*, '*Hasdieu*'; '*Je ne peux pas me r'aspeler pourquoi je vous "es-kkris"*' (I can't ree-member why I'm rye-ting to you); and so on and wearingly on. And then there are the drawings. Proust's manuscripts regularly feature marginal doodles (ambiguous figures that often take rather phallic form; female faces in profile with beak-like noses; birds; bicycles). His letters to Hahn contain sketches of stained-glass windows, some he playfully invents, others he had read about in the work of Emile Mâle, others still he saw on his motor car trips from Cabourg.[1] Hahn was more robust than Proust and Anna de Noailles (he lived until 1947) but like Anna he was a kindred artistic spirit, a sounding board, a soothing presence (through his music) even while his blossoming career as a performer, conductor and composer frequently distanced him from Marcel. Although they could never take Mme Proust's place in Marcel's affections, Noailles and Hahn between them went some way towards making Proust's life bearable in the difficult years immediately following her death.

Come August, decisions – not Proust's strong suit – had to be made: where would he go? Brittany? Touraine? Germany? In the end he opted for Cabourg (like the boulevard Haussmann apartment, this was a place familiar to his mother and grandmother) and he would return there annually for the next eight years. The trip brought an unexpected burst of activity: the change of air seemed to do him good and soon he was speeding around the region in a taxicab of the Unic company, run by Proust's old schoolfriend

Jacques Bizet. In 1900, the year of Ruskin's death and Proust's trips to Venice, there were only an estimated 3,000 cars on France's roads. By 1910 this number had risen to 54,000 and the realms of possibility for the traveller were radically changed.[2] Fortified by heroic quantities of caffeine (to keep, he believed, his asthma at bay) Proust travelled in a car driven by Alfred Agostinelli, a handsome nineteen-year-old from Monaco, born to an Italian father and a mother from Nice. With this swift and readily accessible means of transport Proust was able to visit churches, cathedrals and other sites of interest. Places read and dreamed about could be seen, carved figures contemplated in sunshine and in shade, rather than solely on the unchanging surface of the page. For one so used to stasis and enclosure as Proust, these trips were wholly invigorating. The sense of speed garnered from automotive travel required a complete recalibration of his sense of time, space and distance. He explores the experience in 'Impressions de route en automobile' ('Impressions of Travel in a Motor Car'), published in November 1907; this is an essay on perspective and perception, asking questions similar to those raised by the early Cubist art of Braque and Picasso, whose disruptive, provocative figures of *Les Demoiselles d'Avignon* (1907) had just been completed in the Spaniard's Paris studio. But Proust's essay is a celebration of modernity as under- stood by a fledgling traveller whose points of reference are in Ruskin, seventeenth-century Dutch landscape painters and the music of Wagner. The experience upon which the essay is based clearly made a profound impression on Proust, since the illusion, seen from Agostinelli's taxi, of the dance of the apparently mobile steeples of the churches of Saint-Etienne and Saint-Pierre on the approach to Caen, caused by the speed of the car and the turns in the road, is lifted and transposed into a key scene in *Swann's Way*: the narrator's joy while travelling towards Martinville in Dr Percepied's carriage as a boy is the basis for his first (and, for a long time, only) foray into writing. Crucially, the passage reappears later in 'The Fugitive', printed in *Le Figaro*: the narrator's first published article and a sign that perhaps – just perhaps – he may have it in him to become a writer.

Such were undoubtedly Proust's hopes as 1908 rolled round. When writing to thank Mme Straus for her New Year gift of five little notebooks he intimated his desire 'to settle down to quite a long piece of work' (*Corr.*, VIII, 39), a remark which, in retrospect, we might nominate as one of literary history's greatest understatements. In one of these notebooks, known as the *Carnet de 1908*, Proust began to jot ideas, brief sketches of characters or situations, lists of pages he had drafted, and notes from his reading of the time. The *Carnet*, to which Proust continued adding until 1912, is an invaluable

Proust's *carnets*.

document for our understanding of the genesis of *A la recherche* and how it coalesced out of the hybrid project known as *Against Sainte-Beuve*.

Before Sainte-Beuve, and before the nascent novel, however, came a final stage in Proust's apprenticeship: the pastiche. In January 1908 a news story broke that reads nowadays like an Ealing comedy: Henri Lemoine, an engineer employed by the De Beers company, duped its president into believing he had perfected a technique of manufacturing diamonds. On the strength of his claim (bolstered with impressive chutzpah, including a laboratory demonstration performed naked so as to 'prove' he was not cheating) he swindled, over a period of three years, a substantial sum from De Beers, only to be caught out when a jeweller revealed he had sold Lemoine the diamonds the latter had claimed to have created synthetically. For a writer with Proust's playful sense of humour the scope for comic exploitation offered by this tale could not be resisted. On 22 February the literary supplement of *Le Figaro* printed the first run of his brilliant pastiches – scenes from the Lemoine affair written in the style of Balzac, the Goncourt brothers, the historian Michelet and the critic Emile Faguet. Others (of Flaubert, Sainte-Beuve and Renan) appeared in March. Their virtuosic accomplishments are quite remarkable: each one demonstrates Proust's exceptional ear, his ability to replicate the tone, the stylistic traits – the writerly fingerprint – of a particular author. Proust viewed them as an entertainment but also as 'literary criticism in action' (*Corr.*, VIII, 61); he described his practice in terms of music, explaining to Robert Dreyfus that for the pastiche of Renan he 'had set [his] inner metronome' to Renan's rhythm and 'could have written ten volumes like that' (*Corr.*, VIII, 67). In 1919 he recognized the pastiches, which were widely celebrated as masterly, for what they were: 'a matter of hygiene . . . necessary to purge oneself of the most natural vice of idolatry and imitation' (*Corr.*, XVIII, 380). Actively he reproduced the voices of his forebears better to be able to avoid involuntary pastiche, a problem to which lesser writers are often prey. As his own voice grew stronger within him, as the notes in the *Carnet* accumulated, his sensitivity to the words of others grew ever more acute. He railed against the unthinking recourse to cliché that he found choking a review of the letters of Georges Bizet, the first husband of his beloved Mme Straus: 'why is Paris immediately qualified as "the great city", Delaunay "the master painter" . . . ?' Such platitudes must be resisted: each writer worthy of the name, Proust counters, 'is obliged to make for himself his own language', since 'only that which can bear the mark of our choice, our taste, our uncertainty, our desire, and our weakness, can be beautiful' (*Corr.*, VIII, 276–8). These words are articulated with assurance, ambition and humility – traits that will characterize the writing that would cement his place as the greatest prose stylist of his generation.

The *Carnet de 1908* has been a revealing source for scholars: it is a logbook of Proust's progress, a net to catch the thoughts that thronged his restless mind. Some of these were rejected and thrown back into the swell, but most were mobilized in the flow of writing and rewriting that coursed from Proust's pen from 1908 to 1912 and beyond. Often the briefest telegraphic notes contain in embryo scenes that we can recognize in the finished novel. The line '*Cabourg marcher sur les tapis en s'habillant, soleil dehors Venise*' (Cabourg walking on the carpets while getting dressed, sun outside Venice), for example, which is more Gertrude Stein than Marcel Proust, draws together two distant locations via two sensory experiences – the sensation of carpet underfoot and the quality of the sunlight beyond the window.[3] Similar connections and reawakenings will occur in *Time Regained* when a starched napkin recalls the towel with which the adolescent narrator dried his face during his first stay in Balbec (Cabourg in the *Carnet* eventually gives way to the fictional Balbec, but only after being 'Querqueville', 'Briquebec' and 'Criquebec') and the uneven paving stones of the Guermantes' courtyard beneath his feet transport him back to St Mark's Square in Venice.

Just ten pages into the *Carnet* he writes the following:

> Maybe I should bless my ill health, which has taught me, by the ballast of fatigue, immobility and silence, the possibility of work. The presages of death. Soon you will not be able to say all of that. Laziness or doubt or impotence taking refuge in the uncertainty regarding the form of art. Should I write a novel, a philosophical study, am I a novelist?[4]

Pondering his vocation, already in 1908 Proust was concerned by 'the presages of death'. He is charged with a desire (just like the narrator at the close of *Time Regained*) to say his piece before it is too late. And this would be a recurring concern for him in the years to come. Later in 1908 he wrote to Georges de Lauris, quoting the Gospel of John, somewhat altered, via Ruskin (there are very few straight lines in Proust): 'Work while you still have light', writes Proust (in the gospel, Jesus says 'walk while you have the light, lest darkness overtake you'; John 12:35). 'As I no longer have it', he continues, 'I am setting myself to work' (*Corr.*, VIII, 316). And there was a good deal of it to do.

To Albufera in early May Proust gave an intriguing rundown of his work in progress. 'I have under way', he states

A study of the nobility
A Parisian novel
An essay on Sainte-Beuve and Flaubert
An essay on women
An essay on pederasty (not easy to publish)
A study on stained-glass windows
A study on tombstones
A study on the novel (*Corr.*, VIII, 112–13)

If illustration were needed of the multifariousness of Proust's thought or indeed the rich diversity of the soil from which *A la recherche* grew, this is it. It is no surprise that frequently in his letters of this time we find Proust apologizing to his correspondents for mislaying letters he has written or received, repeating messages already conveyed and writing *post scriptum* messages intended for one missive on the foot of another being drafted at the same time. His mind was like a cabinet of curiosities, his pen a virtuoso composer improvising a sort of polyphony or fugue amid his phials and fumigations. In his list of work ongoing are found most of the dominant concerns of *A la recherche du temps perdu*: society, genealogy, mortality, gender and sexuality, desire, art, memorialization. And this is the first mention of an essay on Sainte-Beuve, although six months later the essay still did not exist in material form. (Flaubert's style would be the subject of a late essay published in 1920.) From Anna de Noailles and Georges de Lauris Proust sought advice about how to proceed. He wanted to write a study on Sainte-Beuve that 'is constructed in my mind in two different ways between which I must choose'. The first is classic in form, 'like an essay by Taine but less good'. The second starts with 'the story of a morning, Maman would come to my bedside and I would tell her about an article that I want to do on Sainte-Beuve. And I would expand on it for her' (*Corr.*, VIII, 320–21). The idea presented here of writing a critical work in the form of a fictionalized dialogue, or at least a framed monologue, is innovative. We might also note that the anticipated hybrid form permits the resurrection of his mother, just as 'Impressions of Travel in a Motor Car' ends with an imagined homecoming to his open-armed parents. Proust was starting to write his future but he still hankered after his past.

July and August were spent in Cabourg, travelling again in Agostinelli's taxi and also that of Odilon Albaret, who subsequently joined Proust's service as his driver. Cabourg afforded Proust the opportunity to observe holidaymakers, bourgeois and upper crust alike. Social mores fascinated him, and not just those of the grand salons he frequented in Paris: he was as likely to be found playing dominoes and gossiping with Agostinelli and Nicolas Cottin as he was placing bets or talking with other guests in the casino. Matters of money – betting and speculating on the stock market – began to interest Proust more and more around this time. Despite having inherited a position of financial security, Proust was frequently concerned about his levels of solvency and sought to shore up his position buying and selling shares. He was not, however, particularly market-savvy and reading his correspondence with his financial advisor Lionel Hauser (1868–1958), who worked for the Warburg Bank, one gets a sense that it was the magic of the names of companies that steered Proust's decisions, rather than Hauser's diligent, amiable advice. Marcel had written with sadness to Fénelon in 1906 that he had the desire to travel but judged the fulfilment of this desire to be impossible (*Corr.*, vi, 267). The circle of his actual movements was ever diminishing but in his stock dealings with Hauser he travelled the world, from the railway companies of Mexico and Tanganyika to Australian Gold Mines, Royal Dutch Petroleum and Rio de Janeiro Tram, Light and Power. His investments were seldom lucrative and at times brought him closer to financial trouble than he would have been without them, but like so many things that Proust enjoyed from a distance, they let him dream.

In Cabourg Proust associated with a number of young men. There was Agostinelli, who turned twenty in October 1908; Albert Nahmias, who was twenty-two and later served as Proust's secretary; and through the Vicomte Charles d'Alton, a friend Proust made at the hotel, he became acquainted with Marcel Plantevignes, a nineteen-year-old, with whom he took the air and talked at length in his room. One day, however, a woman unknown to Proust had words with Plantevignes, voicing concern at his devoting so much time to a man thought to be a homosexual (this was at the height of the Eulenberg trials in Germany, which stirred memories of those of Oscar Wilde in 1895). Plantevignes simply said nothing and this wounded Proust deeply. He felt like he had been 'stabbed in the back' by someone who had 'clumsily wasted a friendship which could have been very beautiful' (*Corr.*, VIII, 208). All of these men were in the prime of their youth; as Proust said of Plantevignes, their very spirit was 'still in bloom' (*encore en fleur*; *Corr.*, VIII, 221), using a phrase that would come to qualify the young girls first met at Balbec who give his finished novel's second volume its title – *A l'ombre des jeunes filles en fleurs* (literally 'in the shadow of young girls in flower'). Critics have long suggested that Proust's girls are simply young men in drag, that Albertine is little more than an Albert or an Alfred in a skirt. While it would be short-sighted to argue that Proust's experiences with these men at Cabourg (and his friendships at the *lycée* and during his later studies) are irrelevant in his depiction of the amorous goings on in Balbec, to suggest a simple transposition of one gender for the other is vastly to underestimate Proust's powers as an observer and a writer. His curiosity, his passionate urge to taxonomize and above all to *understand* are inimical to the notion that his novel might simply be *about* desire and love between men, just as his creative talent as a writer makes it absurd to argue for one-for-one equivalences between his flesh-and-blood acquaintances and the characters that inhabit his pages.[5]

The more we learn about Proust's life, of course, the more we come to realize that practically every scrap of his experience nourished the book that began to take shape in 1908. In October that year, for example, he sent a telegram to Robert de Billy, conveying his sympathies for Billy's wife who was ill, except the functionary at the telegram office misread 'Marcel' and the end of the message Billy received read '*Amitiés, Pascal*' (*Corr.*, VIII, 231). The dramatic potentiality of this banal blunder evidently struck a chord with Proust, for in *The Fugitive* the narrator, grieving Albertine's death, receives a telegram in Venice requesting a meeting and a discussion of marriage, signed 'Tenderly, Albertine'. His world is in turmoil until a letter from Gilberte reveals that she had sent the telegram: the operator had deciphered as 'Albertine' the arabesques of Gilberte's handwritten signature. *A la recherche* is concerned throughout its great length with the grandeur of the achievements of the mind; but it equally interrogates what we can learn from mistakes and miscalculations. The mundane in Proust always has its place alongside the monumental and can often prove to be just as revealing and profound.

Late in 1908 Proust purchased a quantity of school notebooks – *cahiers* of the sort he had used at Condorcet – and started to use these to draft his longer fragments. Ten of these would come to be filled with notes that we now know as *Against Sainte-Beuve*, but this title occludes the presence of a good deal of material preparatory for *A la recherche* and actually unrelated to Sainte-Beuve. There are, in fact, two competing editions of *Contre Sainte-Beuve*, which reflect the different directions in which a reading of the material may lead. Bernard de Fallois' original edition, first published in 1954 and still in print in the Folio 'Essais' collection, gathers much (including 75 loose sheets that have since disappeared) that is novelistic and has little to do with a critical discussion of Sainte-Beuve and his methods. Indeed, a good deal of this material is in fact published in the '*Esquisses*' (Drafts) section of the most recent scholarly edition of *A la recherche* published by the Bibliothèque de la Pléiade. In 1971 an alternate critical edition of *Contre Sainte-Beuve* appeared, prepared for the Pléiade by Pierre Clarac, whose method was to privilege the critical, essayistic material and to eschew that which was narrative or dialogical. The complexity of this editorial task is testament to the competing directions taken by Proust's writing in 1908–9.

In early 1909 (just days before the publication in *Le Figaro* of Marinetti's 'Futurist Manifesto', proclaiming the primacy of speed, recklessness and energy), Proust was suffering 'incessant attacks'

(*Corr.*, IX, 23) that slowed him down and reduced the time during which he was able to write. A final Lemoine pastiche (of Henri de Regnier), however, did appear on 6 March. Shortly after this he wrote to Lauris that there would be no more pastiches but there was a chance that his study of Sainte-Beuve would appear 'because this full trunk in the middle of my mind is bothering me and I need to decide whether to set off or to unpack it' (*Corr.*, IX, 61). The posthumous editorial history of *Against Sainte-Beuve* shows that this image is not quite apposite: Proust was folding his ideas now into a trunk stamped 'novel', now into one stamped 'essay'; and sometimes, like a long garment laid across both containers on which the lids are then shut, his writing spanned both genres at once but was cinched or pulled out of shape by the pressure of the containers.

By June Proust was able to announce progress ('I am right in the midst of it', he wrote to Lauris, 'and what's more, it's hateful'; *Corr.*, IX, 116), but like the endurance athlete whose coping strategy with pain is simply to push on harder, Proust did not slow down. For a period in early July he neither slept nor switched off his light for more than 60 hours (*Corr.*, IX, 134); the end result of such marathon sessions was approximately 700 pages of manuscript notes. Through these pages flit scenarios, places and characters we will come to know under other names in *A la recherche*. We encounter the *côté de Méséglise* and the *côté de Villebon*, the first of which is also known as Swann's way in the novel, the second being a precursor to the Guermantes way (between 1908 and 1910 Proust repeatedly asked Lauris to find out if anyone of this name was still alive, if it was 'usable' without causing offence). A nobleman, the Marquis de Guercy is a forerunner of Charlus; another, Montargis, foreshadows Saint-Loup. And a forgotten moment of the past is recalled when consuming not a *petite madeleine* with his mother but some toast and tea provided by an elderly cook (at least six different versions of the scene shuffle the variables before the 'squat, plump little cakes' take pride of place; *Swann's Way*, 51; I, 44).

Away from the notes that adumbrate the novel, Proust's critical wrangle with Sainte-Beuve was concurrently developed. Sainte-Beuve was a major voice of the French literary establishment for the generation preceding Proust's. His critical method advocated knowledge of a writer's biography and worldly dealings in order to appreciate his or her works. Sainte-Beuve's weekly column in *Le Constitutionnel*, entitled 'Causeries' ('Talk', or 'Chatter'), encapsulated for Proust the superficial level on which the critic engaged with his material. In addition, Proust found him to be a mediocre manipulator of the French language and a critic who seldom put his finger on the most salient issues of a text. Proust's notes on Alfred de Musset, Baudelaire and Thomas Hardy (to name just three) in the *Carnet de 1908* reveal him to be the patient, sensitive, close reader he laments Sainte-Beuve as never having been.

During his periods of intense writing Proust often consumed little more than coffee, but shortly after the time of his 60-hour stint, we find in his correspondence a brief note addressed to Céline Cottin revealing that more substantial fare did at times contribute to his sustenance.

> Céline, I send you hearty compliments and thanks for the marvellous *bœuf mode*. I should like to succeed as well as you in what I am going to do tonight; I would like my style to be as clear, as firm as your jelly – my ideas to be as tasty as your carrots and as nourishing and fresh as your meat. As I await the completion of my work, I congratulate you on yours. (*Corr.*, IX, 139)

With his eye trained by Ruskin, Proust recognized the work of the artisan wherever he encountered it. The humility in these lines is striking: the master takes a model of success from his subaltern's endeavours in the kitchen and strives to match it with his pen. In his novel, Proust pays a double homage to Céline: when Françoise prepares the same, sublime dish for the diplomat

Norpois, a revered guest (*Budding Grove*, 18; I, 437), the narrator likens the cook's search for the perfect ingredients in Les Halles to Michelangelo's pilgrimages to Carrara to identify the ideal blocks of marble for his statue of Julius II. Later, in *Time Regained*, when the narrator seeks to articulate how he will construct the novel he finally feels ready to write he uses the culinary accomplishment to explain his creative principles: any place, person or event in a book is made up from 'numerous impressions' derived from a multitude of sources: thus his book should be made 'in the same way that Françoise made that *bœuf à la mode* which M. de Norpois had found so delicious, just because she had enriched its jelly with so many carefully chosen pieces of meat' (*Time Regained*, 434; IV, 612).

By August 1909 Proust had the confidence in what he had produced to contact Alfred Vallette, director of the *Mercure de France*, who had published his work on Ruskin:

> I am finishing a book which, despite its provisional title, *Contre Sainte-Beuve, Souvenir d'une matinée* [*Against Sainte-Beuve, Memory of a Morning*], is a real novel and one which is extremely indecent in places. One of the main characters is a homosexual ... The book ends with a long conversation on Sainte-Beuve and on aesthetics ... and when you finish it, you'll see, I hope, that the whole novel is but a putting into action of the principles of art that are expressed in that final part, a sort of preface if you like placed at the end. (*Corr.*, IX, 155–6)

This summary reveals that in just over seven months since his queries regarding form to Lauris and Anna de Noailles, the project has taken shape as a novel, albeit an unconventional one. Its form – concluding with a sort of monologue-essay on the work's 'principles of art' – bears some resemblance to *A la recherche*, whose aesthetic principles are expounded at length in the library scene in *Time Regained*; and the central, homosexual figure indicates that already the role of Guercy/Charlus was deemed to be key. Proust wished Vallette to publish the novelistic part in fortnightly instalments in his journal, the *Mercure de France*, and then, in January or February 1910, to publish the full volume, the novelistic part completed by the critical conversation. Vallette would not commit, however, and the problem that plagued Proust's composition and editing throughout his life was already beginning to show: to Mme Straus he wrote later in August that he had 'started – and finished – a whole long book' but that he wanted 'properly to finish, to get to the end', adding 'If everything is written, a lot of things need to be reworked' (*Corr.*, IX, 157, 163). The novel of 1909, which was typed up in October and November, would be a substantial volume of more than 400 pages, but its shape was still somewhat indeterminate.

Proust continued to see his health as 'a formidable obstacle' (*Corr.*, IX, 196) to his work, and a plangent letter written on returning to Paris at the end of the summer gives a stark reminder of his vulnerability, even a time of great productivity. He had suffered a painful dental abscess and worried about future complications; his asthma showed little sign of fading; 'I'm scared', he wrote frankly to Lauris. 'How can I live like this without being able to work, see anyone, eat, breathe?' (*Corr.*, IX, 191). It is true that his social engagements had fallen away significantly in the space of the last year but in November he hired three boxes at the Théâtre des Variétés where he introduced his young male friends from Cabourg to his older companions, including Emmanuel Bibesco, Lauris, Fénelon and Reynaldo. They watched a performance of Feydeau and Croisset's new play *Le Circuit*, perhaps the first dramatic work to centre on motor cars, their drivers and passengers, a work reflecting the fascination with speed heralded by Marinetti's manifesto.

Around this time Proust read his first 200 pages to Reynaldo, who responded positively. Buoyed by this and encouraging comments from Lauris, Proust sent the freshly prepared typescript of his first three notebooks to *Le Figaro*. When they met in Cabourg in

August, Gaston Calmette had offered to serialize the novel in his paper but due to a misunderstanding (largely of Proust's creation), the typescript remained at the *Figaro* offices, unread by Calmette, until Proust himself made a rare trip out in early July 1910 to retrieve it. Proust's existence was highly sedentary and if this made him feel trapped, the freak flooding of Paris in late January, which reached the front door of 102 boulevard Haussmann and inundated the cellar, did nothing to ease his nerves. Nor did the noise of the repairs and restoration work that were required once the waters receded. In March, however, he was able to attend a dinner *chez* Straus where he met a young poet, Jean Cocteau (1889–1963), who became a major figure in the Paris avant-garde and one of twentieth-century France's most multi-talented (and relentlessly self-promoting) artists. Soon, however, Proust's ill health tightened its grip: the smallest things, such as getting up for an hour, took vast amounts of energy and preparation. Late April and early May were marked by emphysema, bronchitis and fever. 'If I can only delay dying until I have fulfilled my principal intellectual and sentimental vows!' he wrote to Mme Straus during this dark time, 'For I do not have, or no longer have, any others' (*Corr.*, x, 79).

As always, his ailments ebbed and flowed: by June Proust managed to go out once more to take his place as an enraptured spectator at the Opéra for the Ballets Russes production of Fokine's *Cléopâtre*, *Les Sylphides* and *Scheherazade*. Here was an artistic event that caressed and assaulted the senses, where, against decors by Léon Bakst, Nijinsky and Ida Rubinstein performed Fokine's choreography to music by Rimsky-Korsakov, Mussorgsky and Chopin among others. Proust may have been administering himself caffeine, trional and a range of other treatments, but the combinatory power of artistic energies, colours, the sheer boldness of spirit of the Ballets Russes provided holistic therapy of a most welcome sort.

With this shot in the arm Marcel felt well enough to depart for Cabourg. During his absence he had the walls of his boulevard

Haussmann bedroom lined with cork, an attempt to insulate himself from the noise that so importuned him. This move is prized by the 'did you know Albert Camus was a goalkeeper?' school of literary anecdote; it was eccentric, perhaps, but relatively un-extravagant by Proust's standards, particularly in the days before modern soundproofing and double-glazing. Although the sea air was supposed to do him good, successive annual visits to Cabourg at the same time of year merely emphasized to Proust the realization of how his health had diminished over the last four years. His movements had shrunk from regular motor car expeditions to walks on the beach, to strolls around the hotel. In the summer of 1910 he managed to set foot on the beach only once in more than two months in Cabourg (*Corr.*, x, 215) and so, alert to his frailty and to the ticking of the clock, Proust returned to his much touted cork-lined room in October 1910.

The following February a new innovation brought some light into his life: the Théâtrophone, using telephone technology, allowed subscribers to listen live from the comfort of their home to concerts and opera performances taking place in Paris. For Proust this was a boon; a particular favourite was Debussy's opera *Pelléas et Mélisande* (1902), based on Maeterlinck's symbolist drama, to which he first listened on 21 February and by which he was, for a time, wholly captivated. The pleasures of the new technology were fleeting, however. 'I have lost all those I loved,' he wrote to Louis de Robert in March, 'my health is definitively ruined and it has now been ten years that I have been bedridden, getting up for a few hours once a month, never opening a window or a shutter' (*Corr.*, x, 271). Bedridden, but not unproductive. Shortly after the first hearing of *Pelléas*, Proust suggested to Lauris that his book might 'with a bit of nerve be ready in two months' (*Corr.*, x, 254), yet at Cabourg, almost five months later, he wrote to an unknown young man explaining that 'to finish my novel, it would be useful to me to have, for two or three months, a secretary'. He noted that the book he was completing was 'an extremely considerable work, at least in terms of its mad length' (*Corr.*, x, 307–8). His request was not accepted but fortunately the Grand Hotel had the services of a typist, an Englishwoman named Cecilia Hayward, whom Proust engaged to make legible the handwritten fruits of his nocturnal labours: this amounted to just over 700 pages of typescript – a considerable work indeed, but only the beginning of the novel as we know it today.

These pages, typed by Miss Hayward from the *cahiers* kept in order by Albert Nahmias, whose relation with Proust grew closer in 1911, are the basis for the first galley proofs for the novel prepared in 1913. While the 'novel of 1909' was a single volume, the 'novel of 1911' was a work of more substantial proportions, comprising a complete version of 'Combray', 'Swann in Love' and 'Place Names: The Name', all this in typescript. Proust's efforts had also yielded draft material for a second substantial volume: made up of scenes involving Bergotte and Elstir, Charlus and the Verdurin clan, the death of the grandmother and the concluding pages of *Time Regained*.[6] Proust's novel now had a beginning and an ending. But would it find a publisher?

6

# *Swann* Published and Alfred *Disparu*

If, as Proust hoped, his book was to reach 'into the greatest possible number of minds susceptible to receiving it' (*Corr.*, XII, 98), many practical issues needed to be resolved. What preoccupied him most in 1912 and 1913 with regard to his novel was not whether he would find a publisher (of this he seemed confident), but rather questions of shape, scale and nomenclature. How many volumes would there be? Would there be an overarching title? Should multiple volumes be numbered or bear individual titles? What would the titles be? What was the optimal number of lines per page? And pages per volume? Although his health was poor Proust seemed to have endless reserves of stamina when it came to worrying, terrier-like, at these questions, yet they were far from being his only concern. While correcting Miss Hayward's typescript, Proust carried on drafting new material. He worked on an early version of the 'Bal de têtes' ('Masked Ball') section of *Time Regained*: some of this had existed since 1909 and drew on his experiences of going out into the world after long absences (following his mother's death and his own ill health) and finding his acquaintances aged, changed by time. Another sequence, referred to in his notes as 'L'Adoration perpétuelle' ('Perpetual Adoration'), was also developed and would precede the 'Bal de têtes': these pages are an evolved form of the conversation on aesthetics that was going to conclude *Against Sainte-Beuve*. Now, as Tadié has summarized, in draft form Proust had accounts of the experience of Time in both 'positive' or 'pure' form, as tasted in a succession of experiences of involuntary memory that will introduce the 'Perpetual Adoration' scene in the library, and 'negative' or destructive form, as evinced by Time's work on the aged faces of his contemporaries in the 'Bal de têtes'.[1] The book's closing sentence, which ends '*dans le Temps*' (in Time) and brings us full circle from the novel's opening ('*Longtemps . . .*', 'for a long time'), was not formulated just yet, but the radical, spiralling structure – stretching from perceived loss and uncertainty to recollection and recovery – was in place.

Between the summer of 1912 and the spring of 1913 Proust completed a draft of what would be advertised in the 1913 edition of *Swann's Way* as the second volume in a projected trilogy, formed of material that, when the war interrupted publication, became distributed primarily between the volumes published as *Within a Budding Grove* (1919) and *The Guermantes Way* (1921). It is well known that Proust drew extensively on his own experiences in the production of his novel. But as his outings, visits and his hours spent in an upright position diminished, how did the fragile night owl gather and marshal the material required for his massive undertaking?

In large part he did what he knew best: he wrote. A card thanking Albert Henraux for his New Year's wishes is an opportunity to ask which flowers there are at the start of spring around Florence, whether merchants sell them in the open air on the Ponte Vecchio, how they might differ from those found in Paris or in the Beauce and whether there are frescos in Santa Maria del Fiore (*Corr.*, XI, 21). The piece Proust published in *Le Figaro* in March 1913 entitled 'Vacances de Pâques' ('Easter Holidays') as a prepublication taster for his novel shows where these questions were leading: it features material relating to the narrator's dreams of travel subsequently reworked and integrated into *Swann's Way* and *The Guermantes Way*. Writing in July 1912 to Mme Gaston de Caillavet (this time for clarifications regarding dressmaking and women's fashions), he explained that if an experience had made on him an impression (an important term in Proust's aesthetics) 'to explain it [he] must have exact words.' If he does not know them, he says, 'I leaf through books about botany, or books about architecture, or fashion journals' (*Corr.*, XI, 157). Lucien Daudet confirmed years later that in order to complete 'a magnificent page of *Sodom and Gomorrah*' Proust read the entirety of Darwin's *The Power of Movement in Plants* (1880), evidence of what Daudet called Proust's yearning 'not to leave anything to chance'.[2] His inquiries were not solely book-based, though. Writing to Max Daireaux, an engineer turned poet and novelist whose acquaintance Proust had made in Cabourg, ostensibly to thank him for his most recent book, Proust cannot help but seek advice on 'a few scientific things that have troubled me in the correction of my book'. He then launches into queries about the maturation of eggs (and whether a change in their density as they develop could cause them to move); the rising of the sun; architectural terminology; perspective; the properties of glass . . . Fortunately, Proust did realize how his impulsive inquiries had hijacked proceedings: 'there is something irresistible about the depressing comedy of this letter', he wrote wryly, 'which should be about your book and is about mine' (*Corr.*, XII, 206). A letter the following month mentions his 'interminable correspondence' with 'horticulturists, dressmakers, astronomers, specialists in heraldry, pharmacists' (*Corr.*, XII, 254). Although he kept up the niceties of his personal correspondence (and a vast one at that), the deeper Proust got into *A la recherche* the more frequently his letters served his creative needs, acting as virtual gangways between the outside world and the darkened room in which his novel was steadily maturing.

With the assistance of Albert Nahmias and Miss Hayward, now in Paris, Proust was correcting typescript and drafting new material, often through the night. On 21 March 1912 *Le Figaro* published pages from 'Combray' under the heading (which Proust did not choose) 'On the Threshold of Spring'. This first public taste of the novel was, like subsequent prepublication tasters appearing in June ('Ray of Sunshine on the Balcony') and September ('The Village Church'), not a straightforward excerpt but a careful montage of passages assembled and shaped for the purpose. Reynaldo Hahn's mother died on 25 March, but Proust's recurring asthma attacks prevented him from attending the funeral. The following month, in a letter franked on 15 April, the day that the *Titanic* sank in the North Atlantic, Proust was proclaiming his discomfort to Robert Dreyfus: '*Quel ennui*', he groaned (what a pain it is), 'to be ill and not to be able even to hold a pen!' (*Corr.*, XI, 101). Three weeks later he thought he would be able to receive Dreyfus but could not guarantee to be on form for his friend when, as he put it, he was 'haggard and dosed up with caffeine to this degree' (*Corr.*, XI, 123).

By October 1912 Proust had more or less decided on *Le Temps perdu* and *Le Temps retrouvé* as the titles for what he thought at the time would be a two-volume work, but he could not settle on the overall title *Les Intermittences du cœur* (*The Intermittencies of the Heart*). Earlier in the year Proust wrote to Hahn to sound him out – how different things might have been: *The Stalactites of the Past*; *Reflections in the Patina*; *The Reflections of the Past*; *The Visitor from the Past*; *Reflections of Time*; *Mirrors of the Dream* (*Corr.*, XI, 151). He was clearly determined to convey the centrality of a relation to the past, but the mawkish tone of many of these possible titles is rather more in keeping with *Pleasures and Days* than with the novel as we know it. All were rejected, as was another suggestion, *Gardens in a Cup of Tea*, made later to Louis de Robert (*Corr.*, XII, 232).

Before arriving at a title that would stick, Proust rallied for two final trips of note in 1912. On 4 June he managed to adapt his hours to permit a visit to an exhibition of 29 'admirable Monets' (*Corr.*, XI, 141), the fruits of the painter's trip in the late autumn of 1908 to Venice, whose canals and architecture, suffused in the city's enchanting light, feature so prominently in the second half of the

'Albertine cycle' (the material that would become *La Prisonnière* and *La Fugitive – Albertine disparue*) that Proust would first draft between 1914 and 1915. This break from his nocturnal regime was, of course, in the service of his novel. 'I don't know yet if I'll go to Cabourg', he wrote to Armand de Guiche on 7 August, 'I don't think so, but I am impulsive because I am indecisive; when I can no longer bear the weight of my indecision, I leave so as to suffer no longer' (*Corr.*, XI, 172). And so, impulsively, that very day, with Albert Nahmias and Nicolas Cottin, Proust set out for his annual trip to Cabourg. And the impulse seems to have been a good one: improbably, within a fortnight Proust was reporting that he was 'dancing a little every two days so as get the rust from [his] joints' (*Corr.*, XI, 185) and shortly before returning to Paris in mid-September he enjoyed a trip in a motor car with Mme Straus, remembered 'like a sunny enclave in months of darkness' (*Corr.*, XI, 222), to the picturesque village of Honfleur to the west of Cabourg down the Normandy coast, another site prized by Monet among others.

With sea air in his lungs Proust returned to Paris to find a publisher. Calmette, who had published so much of Proust's writing to date in *Le Figaro*, offered some hope. He told Mme Straus that Eugène Fasquelle, the director of the Charpentier publishing house, had 'promised' to publish the novel on Calmette's recommendation. Proust's contemporaries Fernand Gregh, Robert Dreyfus and Louis de Robert had all published between Charpentier covers, as had Flaubert, Zola and the Goncourts, but Fasquelle had refused Proust's offer of a volume of his pastiches in 1908. Proust nevertheless sensed an opportunity and sent Fasquelle his type-script accompanied by a (characteristically) long letter making plain that his book was 'indecent' in parts (which is not immediately clear in the first instalment) and that it would consist of two volumes, *Le Temps perdu* and *Le Temps retrouvé*, under the general title *Les Intermittences du cœur*, although its extent ('around 1,250 very full pages'; *Corr.*, XI, 236) suggested three volumes might be necessary. At the same time, however, he had discussed his work with Antoine Bibesco who contacted Jacques Copeau, director of the *Nouvelle revue française* (NRF), which had an imprint of its own, founded in 1911 and headed by Gaston Gallimard. Attracted by the intellectual standing of the NRF, Proust entered into correspondence with Gallimard, again writing lengthily about the nature of his novel, its need to be subdivided into volumes, how this might be approached, and so on and on. Eventually, in the first week of November, Gallimard offered to visit boulevard Haussmann to collect the typescript himself but Proust turned him down, noting amusingly 'you don't know how heavy it is' (*Corr.*, XI, 285). In this letter he suggests for the first time that if three volumes are required, the second might be entitled *A l'ombre des jeunes filles en fleurs*; he also notes (ever eager, ever unrealistic about practical issues of time) that he would like to see the first volume appear in February 1913 with the second delayed until November that year 'in order to allow the assimilation of such a big chunk to happen normally' (*Corr.*, XI, 286). Such were Proust's wishes, but the typescript remained to be read by both publishers. Moreover the fact remained that multi-volume works were extremely rare in the contemporary publishing scene: the average length of works published by the NRF at the time was just 230 pages and what Proust had in store already swamped this more than five times over.[3]

What happened next has, to some degree, passed into literary legend. It is said that André Gide, to whom Proust's hefty typescript was passed, turned it down for the NRF without even untying the string keeping the parcel together, let alone reading it. And the responses from Fasquelle's reader and, a little later, the reader for another publisher, Ollendorff, doubtless still provide solace to rejected fledgling novelists who encounter the anecdotes as they wait for their big break: even Proust, whose gilded name

adorns the coveted leather spines of the Bibliothèque de la
Pléiade, was kicked unceremoniously to the kerb before reaching
his present standing. Around 23 December Gallimard returned
Proust's typescript to him, making it known that the *NRF*'s imprint
would not publish his novel. The second blow came on Christmas
Eve 1912, when Fasquelle returned his copy with the same message.

'After the utter depression of seeming to drown in fathomless
complications and after irritating feelings of impatience at never
being able to surface – the reader has simply no idea of what it's all
about.' Such were the initial thoughts of Fasquelle's reader, an
author by the name of Jacques Normand who sometimes published, coincidentally, as 'Jacques Madeleine'. Proust did not see
the report – it was communicated to the scholar Henri Bonnet by
Fasquelle's heirs and first published in *Le Figaro littéraire* in 1966.
Normand continued: 'It's impossible to make head or tale of it! . . .
What we have here is in fact a clearly defined pathological case.'[4] In
his covering letter to Fasquelle Proust had described his first volume
as a 'poetic overture', in which there is little action but much
'preparation' of characters and sites that are subsequently revisited
and seen afresh later in the work. For Normand, however, it was
'too long, out of all proportion'; he was somewhat overwhelmed
but did concede, in closing his report, that 'it is impossible not to
see here an extraordinary intellectual phenomenon'.[5] The *NRF*
reception was, if anything, even less charitable.

In her memoir *Monsieur Proust*, Céleste Albaret suggests that
Proust himself told her that the knots on the parcel containing
his typescript had not been untied; if this was so, it may have
been in an effort to defend his wounded pride. In fact, in a humble
letter acknowledging his mistake sent in early January 1914, Gide
admitted to having read just two very brief snatches of the novel.
To his mind, as he put it, Proust was '*un snob, un mondain amateur*'
(a snob, a socialite amateur; *Corr.*, XIII, 50), certainly not someone
whose writings would fit with the avant-garde credentials of the

*NRF*. When he actually stole himself and read the book after its publication, Gide came to acknowledge that 'the refusal of this book will remain the *NRF*'s gravest error – and (for I have the shame of being largely responsible for it) one of the most bitter and remorseful regrets of my life' (*Corr.*, XIII, 50). These admissions meant a good deal to Proust but in December 1912 all he had were two flat rejections and a typescript without a home.

Showing impressive resilience, he did not let his deflation show: in fact, he almost immediately made enquiries with Fasquelle in late December about the publication (again, rejected) of a volume of collected articles; and from Louis de Robert he sought advice on approaching Ollendorff, another publisher, with a request to publish the novel at his (Proust's) own expense. The new year came and Proust sent his manuscript to Alfred Humblot, director at Ollendorff; work continued as normal in the cork-lined room he had earlier termed his 'prison without light' (*Corr.*, XI, 271). He made an exceptional trip out at the end of the month, however, wrapped up in a fur-lined coat over his nightshirt, to stand before Notre-Dame Cathedral's portal of St Anne and gaze upon the statuary which, as he lamented to Mme Straus, the steady everyday traffic of Parisians below seldom pauses to contemplate. This portal, dating from the twelfth century, gives material form to a multitude of biblical figures (principally the kings of Judah), evokes their stories and allows an observer to study artisan workmanship that has stood the test of time. Wrapped up as he had been at his brother's wedding, Proust stood before the portal for two hours: the pages on the Balbec church statuary, deciphered for the unversed narrator by the painter Elstir in *Within a Budding Grove*, bear traces of this vigil and echoes of Emile Mâle's account of the portal in his *Religious Art of the Thirteenth Century*. Perhaps Ollendorff would put Proust's novel into print and give him the chance of surviving through time like the carved figures of Notre Dame?

What stood in his way was Ollendorff's reader, whose response, when it came, was even blunter and more obtuse than that of Normand. 'I may be dense', wrote the reviewer, 'but . . . I cannot understand why a man needs 30 pages to describe how he tosses and turns in his bed before falling asleep.'[6] When Proust received word of the refusal he fumed to Louis de Robert at the short-sightedness of the reader: 'here is a man', wrote Proust, 'who has just had in his hands 700 pages in which you will see a good deal of moral experience, of thought and pain which are not diluted but concentrated, and this is the tone he takes to brush it aside!' (*Corr.*, XII, 77). The decision, however, was final. Such a string of rejections would leave some novelists whimpering over their desks, their confidence painfully bruised. But not Proust: the work was not the problem. Like a fire that can only burn brightly if it has a supply of air, the novel needed an audience whose attention would breathe into its pages the life that it needed.

Proust's last chance was with the publishing house run by Bernard Grasset, an energetic man who, although ten years younger than Proust, was already editor of Giraudoux, François Mauriac and the (now unknown) winner of the Goncourt Prize in 1911, Alphonse de Chateaubriant. Proust's priorities were prompt publication and minimal editorial interference, so offering to publish '*à compte d'auteur*' (at the author's expense) was the most likely route to achieving these goals. Proust wrote in February 1913 to René Blum, whom he had known since 1902 via Antoine Bibesco, and who was a close associate of Grasset. He rehearsed the points he had made at length before to Fasquelle, Gallimard and to Ollendorff, stressing even more that the work was challenging, 'a highly composed whole' (*Corr.*, XII, 82). And it was one for which Proust would pay both the publication and publicity costs: his pecuniary interest was 'less important . . . than the penetration of [his] thought into the greatest possible number of minds susceptible to receiving it' (*Corr.*, XII, 98). The contract with Grasset was signed on 13 March. With this in hand Proust's fastidiousness hit new heights: every detail from character size and margin width to the shininess of the paper were weighed and pondered in his tireless letters to his patient editor. But these were minor details: what mattered now was to see through the transformation of typescript to proof copy to printed volumes that would then begin their own trajectory in the hands of their readers.

Shortly after Proust formalized his agreement with Grasset, Proust's driver, Odilon Albaret, formalized one of his own, marrying Céleste Gineste in the village of Auxillac, in the Languedoc-Roussillon region. She promptly moved to Paris with her husband, but with no experience of life outside the village of her birth, at just 21 she found it difficult to adjust to city life. Odilon mentioned this to Proust and when the first volume of his novel finally appeared in November 1913 he suggested to Odilon that having Céleste hand deliver his dedicated copies to friends and acquaintances might be a way to occupy her and take her mind off her distant home. With the departure of Nicolas and Céline Cottin (with whom Céleste never saw eye to eye) Céleste became part of the household: upon Odilon's mobilization at the outbreak of the war she moved into 102 boulevard Haussmann as Proust's housekeeper and would remain in this position, her life entirely recalibrated to her master's nocturnal regime, until November 1922.

On his visits to Cabourg in 1907 and 1908 Proust had been driven by Odilon and by the handsome young Alfred Agostinelli. The latter disappeared from Proust's horizons until May 1911 when he contacted his ex-passenger to enquire whether Proust might be able to assist in finding theatre work for his partner, Anna, an enquiry that Proust obligingly pursued. Subsequently in the spring of 1913 Agostinelli surfaced once more: he had lost his job and needed work. Odilon was reliable and knew the hours his master kept, and Proust had no need for two drivers; unwilling to turn away the young man who had a place in his affections, however, Proust took him on as a secretary-cum-typist, housing him and Anna (whom Proust believed, incorrectly, to be Agostinelli's wife) in the apartment on boulevard Haussmann. And so, as he later explained to Emile Straus, this couple 'became an integral part of my existence' (*Corr.*, XIII, 228), but it was such for only a short, and highly eventful, time.

His proofs began to arrive for correction, but Proust soon realized that rather than correcting the printer's version of his text he was in large part rewriting it, inserting new material, moving existing sections, 'filling up all the blank spaces I can find, and . . . sticking papers on to the top, the bottom, right and left' (*Corr.*, XII, 132). Such was the state in which Proust was returning the proofs that he offered to pay a supplementary fee to Grasset to cover the costs of the additional sets of proofs that were thus necessitated. Grasset accepted. With this colossal, seemingly ever-increasing task before him, Proust's outings were few and, as became his habit, mostly related to his work. Having tried for a week (and failed) to get well enough to hear the Capet Quartet playing Beethoven's late quartets in December 1912, happiness came in early April 1913 when he managed, despite being 'almost dead' to attend a performance of the famous violinist George Enescu performing Franck's Sonata in A major for piano and violin, a performance that left 'a very great impression', provoking 'huge emotion' (*Corr.*, XII, 147): the piece, as Proust later explained, was among those that inspired the fictional music of Vinteuil that plays such a prominent role throughout *A la recherche*. Indeed, it was around this time that Proust fused two characters in his proofs to create the village piano teacher whose compositions bewitch Swann and the narrator after him: Vington, a naturalist and father of a lesbian daughter, and Berget, a composer, were forged together to give Vinteuil.

Corrected proofs of *Swann's Way*, 1913.

*Intermittences pl. 69*

pourvu que cela me plût et fût agréable à ses parents. Avant le déjeuner, sa mère nous prit à part pour dire à Gilberte que cela ennuyait son père que nous allions au concert ce jour-là. Je répondis que c'était trop naturel, Gilberte resta impassible mais devint d'une pâleur qu'elle ne put cacher, et elle ne dit plus un mot, si bien que quand M. Swann revint, sa femme l'emmena à l'autre bout de la pièce et lui parla à l'oreille. Il appela Gilberte, et l'emmena dans la pièce à côté. On entendait des éclats de voix. Je ne pouvais cependant pas croire que Gilberte, si soumise, si tendre, si sage, lui résistât un jour pareil et pour une cause si insignifiante. Enfin son père sortit en lui disant :

— Tu sais ce que je t'ai dit. Maintenant fais ce que tu voudras.

La figure de Gilberte resta contractée pendant tout le déjeuner. Après le déjeuner nous allâmes dans sa chambre. Puis tout d'un coup, sans une hésitation et comme si elle n'en avait jamais eu:

— Deux heures! mais vous savez que le concert commence à deux heures et demie.

— Et elle dit à son institutrice de se dépêcher.

— Mais, lui dis-je, est-ce que cela n'ennuie pas votre père?

— Pas le moins du monde.

— Cependant, il avait peur que cela ne semble bizarre à cause de cet anniversaire.

— Qu'est ce que cela peut me faire ce que les autres pensent. Je trouve cela grotesque de s'occuper des autres dans les choses de sentiment. On sent pour soi, pas pour le public. Mademoiselle qui a peu de distractions se fait une fête d'aller à ce concert, je ne vais pas l'empêcher pour faire plaisir au public.

— Et elle prit son chapeau.

— Mais Gilberte, lui dis-je en lui prenant le bras,

ce n'est pas pour faire plaisir au public, c'est pour faire plaisir à votre père.

— Vous n'allez pas me faire d'observation, j'espère, me cria-t-elle, d'une voix dure en dégageant vivement son bras.

les Swann ne m'excluaient même pas de leur amitié avec Bergotte qui avait été à l'origine du charme que je leur avais trouvé quand avant même de connaître Gilberte, je pensais que son intimité avec le divin vieillard eût fait d'elle pour moi la plus passionnante des amies si le dédain qu'elle avait ne m'avait pas montré que je... un jour que Gilberte m'avait invité à déjeuner pour aller après nous promener ensemble, ses parents avaient pour convives quelques personnes à qui Mme Swann me présenta, quand tout d'un coup, de la même façon qu'elle venait de dire mon nom, comme si nous étions seulement deux autres invités du déjeuner qui avaient chacun également content de connaître l'autre, elle prononça le nom du doux chantre aux cheveux blancs. Ce nom de Bergotte me fit tressauter comme le bruit d'un revolver qu'on aurait déchargé sur moi, mais instinctivement pour faire bonne contenance je saluai; devant moi, comme ces prestidigitateurs qu'on aper-

coup de feu d'où s'envole une colombe, mon salut n'était rendu par un petit homme rude, jeune, trapu à nez et à barbiche noire. Et j'étais mortellement triste car ce qui venait d'être réduit en poussière, la bourre du revolver qui n'était plus qu'un tas de cendre, c'était le langoureux vieillard dont il ne restait plus rien, c'était aussi la beauté d'une œuvre immense que j'avais pu loger dans l'organisme destiné et sacré que j'avais comme un temple construit expressément pour elle, mais à laquelle aucune place n'était réservée dans le corps trapu, rempli de vaisseaux, d'os, et de ganglions du petit homme à nez camus et à barbiche noire qui était devant moi. livres que j'avais tant aimés, car Swann ayant cru devoir lui dire mon goût pour l'un d'eux, il ne montra pas d'étonnement qu'on eut fait part à lui plutôt qu'à un autre, et ne semblait pas voir à l'effet d'une méprise; mais, emplissant le redingote qu'il plus rien au dîneur prochain et à d'autres réalités importantes, ce ne fut que comme à un épisode révolu de sa vie antérieure, et comme si on lui avait fait allusion à un costume de duc de Guise qu'il aurait mis une certaine année à un bal costumé, qu'il sourit en se reportant à l'idée de ses livres, lesquels aussitôt déchurent pour moi, (entraînant dans leur chute tout la valeur du Beau, de l'univers, de la vie), jusqu'à n'avoir été que quelque médiocre divertissement d'homme à barbiche.

Puis je l'entendis parler, compris, l'impression de M. de Norpois. Il avait en effet un organe bizarre; mais rien n'altère autant les qualités matérielles de la voix que de contenir de la pensée : la sonorité des diphtongues, l'énergie des labiales en sont tout influencées. La diction l'est aussi La sienne me semblait tout

tant entièrement différente de son style, et même les choses qu'il disait de celles qu'il écrivait. Mais la parole humaine sert d'un masque sous lequel elle ne suffit pas à nous faire reconnaître d'abord un visage que nous avons vu à découvert dans le style. Dans certains passages de la conversation, où Bergotte se mettait à parler d'une façon qui ne paraissait pas affectée et déplaisante qu'à M. de Norpois, j'ai été bien long à découvrir une exacte correspondance avec ces parties de ses livres où son style devenait si poétique et musical. Alors il voyait dans ce qu'il disait une beauté plastique indépendante de la signification, et comme la parole humaine est en rapport avec l'âme, mais sans l'exprimer comme fait le style, il avait l'air de parler presque à contre-sens, psalmodiant certains mots et s'il poursuivait sous eux une seule image, les filant sans intervalle comme un même son, avec une fatigante monotonie. De sorte qu'un débit prétentieux, emphatique et monotone était le signe de la qualité esthétique des choses qu'il disait, et l'effet, dans sa conversation de ce même pouvoir qui produisait dans son style la suite des images et la beauté de l'harmonie. J'avais en autant plus de peine à m'en apercevoir tout de suite que ce qu'il disait à ces moments là, précisément parce qu'elles était vraiment de Bergotte n'avaient pas l'air d'être de Bergotte. C'était un foisonnement d'idées précises, non incluses dans ce qu'on appelait le genre Bergotte que beaucoup de chroniqueurs s'étaient appropriés, et cette dissemblance était probablement, vu d'une façon trouble à travers la conversation comme une image derrière un verre fumé, un autre aspect de ce fait que quand on lisait une page de Bergotte, elle n'était jamais ce qu'aurait écrit n'importe lequel de ces plats imitateurs qui pourtant, dans le journal et dans le livre, ornaient leur prose de tant d'images et de pensées «à la Bergotte». Cette différence dans le style venait de ce que «à

It is well known that 1913 was something of an *annus mirabilis* in the creative arts. The Armory Show (featuring works by Braque, Cézanne, Duchamp, Kandinsky, Matisse and Picasso among others, many exhibited in the United States for the first time) attracted a storm of attention in New York. *Swann's Way*, appearing in November, was a late arrival in a year that also saw the publication of D. H. Lawrence's *Sons and Lovers*, Apollinaire's *Alcools* and the extraordinary art object-poem formed by the collaboration of Blaise Cendrars and Sonia Delaunay, the *Prose du Trans-sibérien*. Proust was an enthusiastic supporter of the Ballets Russes and, according to Philip Kolb's chronology (*Corr.*, XIII, 12), he attended another major artistic event of 1913, the notorious premiere on 29 May at the Théâtre des Champs-Elysées of Stravinsky's *Rite of Spring*, a work which boldly challenged musical and choreographic conventions, dining afterwards with Stravinsky and Cocteau. Surprisingly, though, there is no mention of this extraordinary evening in Proust's letters (or, it seems, any other source) to corroborate Kolb's assertion.[7]

Around the time of the furore surrounding *The Rite of Spring*, Proust confirmed to Grasset that he had decided on titles for his novel. The first volume would be entitled *Du côté de chez Swann*, the second *Le Côté de Guermantes* and the overall title *A la recherche du temps perdu*. The die had been cast, and not a stalactite in sight. Another change that had a major impact on the work as a whole was Proust's introduction, around May 1913, of a character by the name of Albertine. Just as Berget and Vington were forged together to form Vinteuil, into Albertine is subsumed a previously conceived character present in the drafts at least since 1909–10, a Dutch girl by the name of Maria, associated with the sites of the troubled trip with Fénelon to Belgium and Holland in 1902. The shape, scope and importance of the 'Albertine cycle' were yet to be conceived; in the late spring and early summer of 1913 Albertine was little more than a name but, as Jean-Yves Tadié puts it, the events that Proust was to live through in the following twelve months 'would modify all the established plans and double, in a totally unforeseen fashion, the dimensions of the work, which would go from 1,500 to 3,000 pages in eight years'.[8]

In the second half of 1913 Proust's correspondence gives repeated indications of a latent discomfort or unease that cannot quite be articulated. Repeatedly he tells his acquaintances that he has '*chagrins*' (troubles) that are wearing him down but does not elaborate on what they might be. His existence is cruel, his health, he insistently points out, is worse than it has ever been: almost a refrain in his letters is the observation that 'I've lost so much weight that you wouldn't recognize me' (*Corr.*, XII, 202, *inter alia*). He claims to have lost 30 kilograms, although this figure must surely have been something of an exaggeration. As he was shedding weight (certainly in part due to his tendency to eat – or pick at – just one meal a day at best) he was toiling with the issue of how to trim back his first volume to fit within publishable limits: 'I can't cut it just as easily as a block of butter', he moaned to Grasset (*Corr.*, XII, 233), who would allow a volume of 520 or 680 pages but, categorically, no more. The longer version was unlikely to attract readers but could end at a suitable point; the shorter version was more viable but the material would need to be tweaked to form an acceptable ending. While seeking a resolution to the problem, Proust left Paris for Cabourg in the company of Nicolas Cottin, Agostinelli and Anna. This company, it seems likely, was the source of his underlying *chagrins*.

They arrived on 26 July; in previous years Proust had stayed on until the very end of the season, when even most of the hotel staff had left the coast, but this stay was not to be an extended one. On 4 August Proust set out for Houlgate in a taxi with Agostinelli (as passengers, both – the latter was no longer his driver). Something happened, though, to change the mood, and Proust announced that they must return to the capital. They had neither packed nor paid the bill at the Grand Hôtel; he and Agostinelli made a brief stop in a café, respectively sending messages to Cottin and to Anna to inform them of the changed plans, then the two men promptly boarded a train and were in Paris that evening. What happened between them – or simply in Proust's feverishly active mind – remains uncertain. In a letter to Charles d'Alton apologizing for not seeing him at Cabourg, Proust claimed that for some days he had been feeling 'the moral and physical necessity of coming back at least for a day or two to Paris', then on the way to Houlgate he explained, '*brusquement mon ennui de ne pas être à Paris m'a repris*' (my trouble at not being in Paris suddenly took over) and he hurried back (*Corr.*, XII, 242). In the same letter, however, he mentions in rather veiled terms a 'delicate situation' in relation to Agostinelli and an unnamed third party known to both Proust and d'Alton. Did Agostinelli reveal a relationship or an acquaintance in the region that Proust could not tolerate? (In *Sodom and Gomorrah* Albertine's revelation that she is intimate with young women the narrator knows to be lesbians precipitates their sudden return from Balbec to Paris and the start of their ill-fated cohabitation.) Or did Proust feel, as he had when alone with Fénelon in Belgium and Holland, an overpowering gloom arising from the intolerable pressures of desires unspoken and urges resisted? Unforthcoming to d'Alton, Proust simply asks his friend not to mention to anyone that Agostinelli is acting as his secretary. Just a few days later in a note to Albert Nahmias, however, Proust is less guarded:

> Avoid speaking about my secretary (ex-driver). People are so stupid that they could see in this (as they saw in our friendship) something pederastic [*quelque chose de pédérastique*]. That would be all the same to me but I would be devastated to do wrong by this boy. (*Corr.*, XII, 249)

Proust's frankness here with Nahmias is intriguing. Just as the woman on the front at Cabourg who whispered in Marcel Plantevignes' ear had soured their friendship, and Jean Lorrain's public insinuations about Proust's relation with Lucien Daudet ended in a duel, now any pleasure he might have drawn from his intimacy with Agostinelli seemed doomed, either for personal reasons he would not – or could not – reveal or because of the threat of an intrusive third party. The details of this episode come to us as through a sheet of sea fog. What is clear, however, is that Proust's suffering – through jealousy, unsatisfied longing, betrayal or fear of calumny – was very acute. As he worried about the object of desire living under his own roof, much as Albertine would be captive in the narrator's apartment, Proust's suffering was teaching him lessons, preparing pages as yet unwritten. As we read towards the close of *A la recherche*, '*le bonheur seul est salutaire pour le corps; mais c'est le chagrin qui développe les forces de l'esprit*' (happiness alone is salutary for the body; but it is unhappiness that develops the force of the mind; *Time Regained*, 267, trans. mod; IV, 484).

The late summer and early autumn months were spent adjusting the proofs and developing draft material. Proust was most keen that his novel be judged on its own terms and not be thought of as a work in the same vein as his now long distant *Pleasures and Days*. He requested with some insistence that terms, damaging by association, such as 'delicate' and 'refined' not be applied to his novel, a real and passionate work to which he '[attached] infinitely more importance . . . than to everything I have done until now' (*Corr.*, XII, 295). As publication approached, however, the clouds of his personal troubles seemed determined not to lift: 'My book appears in a fortnight', wrote Proust to the writer and art critic Jean-Louis Vaudoyer in early November 1913, 'just at the moment when I am so unhappy and cannot feel the joy that I would perhaps have had from seeing it finished and read at another moment' (*Corr.*, XII, 291). Agostinelli's taste for speed, developed behind the wheel of his taxi, had become a desire to pilot a plane (a path which Anna believed would lead to great wealth), and Proust had sought to please him by paying for flying lessons at the Blériot Airfield at Buc, near Paris. Happiness and calm still eluded Proust, however, and the clouds were soon to darken yet further.

> Marcel Proust is lying in his bedroom where the shutters are nearly always closed. The electric light accentuates the matt effect of the face, though two eyes, feverish but shining with life, flash out from beneath the hair falling over his forehead. [He] is still a martyr to ill health but he does not appear so once the writer in him, asked to explain his work, comes to life and speaks.[9]

These words greeted readers of *Le Temps* on 13 November 1913, the day before *Swann's Way* was published: Elie-Joseph Bois had interviewed Proust for the paper and this portrait was the first step in the public mythologizing of the writer as eternal invalid. The novel's critical reception was generally positive but Proust's sentiments could not match those of his supporters: 'even if it did succeed', he wrote to Anna de Noailles, 'I wouldn't be able to take from it any joy since I am too sad at present' (*Corr.*, XII, 336). On 1 December the storm broke: unannounced, Alfred and Anna took flight from boulevard Haussmann; Proust would never see Agostinelli again.

Immediately he made enquiries to his trusted friend Nahmias about the practicalities of having someone followed; how did one contact a private detective? Soon Nahmias himself was sent to seek out Agostinelli who, Proust had discovered, had travelled to Monte Carlo, where his father lived. Proust's approach was to seek to bribe Agostinelli *père* into persuading his son to return to Paris. To Nahmias in Nice and Monte Carlo Proust sent ten telegrams in the space of four days, some of them wildly long, most of them cryptic and some of them signed 'Max Werth', a name assumed for confidentiality. Nahmias' mission, however, came to nought. Readers familiar with *A la recherche* will recognize vestiges of these dramatic events in the pages of *The Fugitive*: when Albertine flees the narrator's apartment to the Touraine, Saint-Loup is sent after her but returns unrewarded.

Proust was left alone, then, to confront his critics. Much to his frustration, shortly after Nahmias' return *Le Temps* published a very negative piece that seemed to undo the good work of the interview with Bois that appeared on the eve of the novel's publication. Paul Souday (like many readers after him, it must be said) felt Proust's novel to be over-long and self-indulgent. It was also full of errors that were clearly typographical but which, he pedantically and insistently suggested, were down to Proust's imperfect knowledge of French. Proust wrote privately to Souday, explaining the typographical nature of the errors and pointing out some in Souday's own piece that did not for a moment make Proust think that he, Souday, did not know his grammar. A tiresome business, to be sure, but some good came of it: Gabriel Astruc, a former proofreader turned founder of the Théâtre des Champs-Elysées, had seen Souday's piece, bought a copy of Proust's novel and, as he read along, had marked out all of the printer's errors he encountered. He was most enthusiastic about the book, corresponded with Proust and, at the author's request, loaned him the corrected copy so that Proust could eradicate the errors from subsequent printings.

With the new year came various sorts of gratification. The letter from Gide in early January, admitting to his grave misjudgement of the quality of Proust's novel, raised the author's spirits. And in early February a bright young critic, Jacques Rivière, part of the *NRF* circle, wrote a letter that thrilled Proust, expressing his great admiration for *Swann's Way*. Rivière recognized the overarching structure, the careful plotting and planning: 'Finally', Proust famously replied, 'I have found a reader who *senses* that my book is a dogmatic work and a construction!' Immediately Proust identifies between them '*une amitié spirituelle*' (a friendship of the mind; *Corr.*, XIII, 98) and it was one that would last the rest of his life. Gide wrote again in March, explaining that the Editorial Board of the NRF had met and agreed with 'enthusiasm and unanimity' to the prospect of publishing the remaining parts of Proust's novel. What did the author think? This matter was complex: Proust felt a strong loyalty to Grasset who had stood by him, obligingly met his requests and coped with his proliferating proofs (Fasquelle too had made a volte-face that Proust turned down); but the intellectual prestige of the NRF was second to none and publication under their imprint was a badge of honour that held for Proust considerable allure. He wished above all to maintain control over his own creation and not to do a good man a disservice. The book was selling steadily, yet Grasset straightforwardly told Proust, as a friend rather than as a businessman, that he would not hold the author to any obligation: Proust should carry on publishing with Grasset because he wanted to, not because of any legal or administrative constraint. This courtesy humbled Proust who decided to stay with Grasset and to offer, as a compromise, prepublication excerpts to the NRF.

In March there occurred an event that troubled Proust deeply. Gaston Calmette, the editor of *Le Figaro* and the dedicatee of *Swann's Way*, had for some time been involved in a fierce campaign in his newspaper's pages against Joseph Caillaux, a left-wing politician and former prime minister. So wrapped up was Calmette in the campaign (culminating in the publication of an incriminating private letter from Caillaux to a former mistress) that he acknowledged neither the Tiffany cigarette case Proust gave him, nor the dedication of *Swann's Way* 'as an expression of profound and affection recognition'. Publishing Caillaux's letter tipped the balance for the politician's wife: Mme Caillaux appeared at the

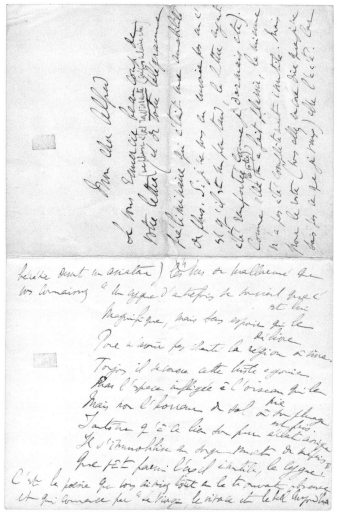

The only extant letter from Proust to Agostinelli, 1914, parts of which resurface in
*Le Fugitive*.

offices of *Le Figaro* concealing a handgun, gained entry to Calmette's office and repeatedly shot him, fatally wounding him. Agostinelli had fled without explanation; Proust's beloved parents were dead and had not witnessed the publication of his novel; Fénelon was a world away at the French embassy in Cuba; and now, one of the few remaining individuals to have shown faith in Proust's abilities had met his fate, never to print or to spike another story again.

If this sudden reminder of mortality was unwelcome to the man who had written fully twelve months earlier to Antoine Bibesco that he was 'nearer death than you think' (*Corr.*, XII, 123), the events of May 1914 would test his mettle even further. From the sole surviving letter between Proust and Agostinelli we can ascertain that they had been writing to each other for a time. Agostinelli, using money Proust had been sending him, had enrolled at a flying school near Antibes (unknown to Proust at the time he had done so under the assumed name 'Marcel Swann'). Proust, still angling for Agostinelli's return, had spent a vast sum of money on a plane for the younger man. Should the order be cancelled? If the plane were kept, Proust would have no use for it, but might have inscribed on its fuselage lines from Mallarmé's sonnet 'Le Vierge, le vivace et le bel aujourd'hui', a poem whose central trope is a swan trapped, flightless, in ice. We will never know the effect of this pathos on Agostinelli: on 30 May, the day Proust sent the letter, the budding pilot set out for his second solo flight after two months' training. He disregarded the warning not to leave the specified flying area and took his plane out over the sea. He swept too low, however, a wingtip caught the water and the monoplane went down. A newspaper report the following day described the wrenching scene of the pilot scrambling out on top of his sinking plane, gesticulating to the helpless observers on the shore before disappearing beneath the waves.

Proust heard about the calamity in a telegram from Anna that evening. Agostinelli's body was not found until 7 June: inside his flight suit was a substantial sum of money (most likely his savings from what Proust had sent). Marcel's inevitable sense of guilt was keenly felt; as he put it to Emile Straus, 'Today I have the trouble [*chagrin*] of thinking that if he had not met me and had not earned so much money from me, he would not have had the means to take up aviation' (*Corr.*, XIII, 228). To Reynaldo, in October, after the immediate pain had dissipated, he expressed his feelings quite simply: 'I truly loved Alfred. It's not enough to say that I loved him, I adored him. And I don't know why I am writing this in the past since I still love him' (*Corr.*, XIII, 311). This troubled relation between the natural passage of time and the differently geared intensity of our emotional attachment to other human beings is one with which we all wrestle at some point in our lives. It features prominently in *Albertine disparue* (*The Fugitive*), a volume that Proust would draft during the next two years, in which love, loss and mourning are examined with a blend of sensitivity and obsessive curiosity that produces pages of emotional intensity and profound beauty unmatched elsewhere in modern literature.

7

# The Great War

The soldiers do their duty; since I can't fight like them, my duty is to write my book, to construct my work. Time presses too much for me to devote myself to anything else.

Letter to Céleste Albaret, September 1914

Calmette's violent death had shaken Proust and the wound inflicted on him by Agostinelli's death was a deep one. When Archduke Franz Ferdinand and his wife were assassinated in Sarajevo, just one month after Agostinelli's demise, a further calamity was triggered that would take on global proportions. Germany declared war on France on 3 August and German troops were within 30 miles of Paris by 2 September, at which point the government retreated to Bordeaux. Just as his pregnant mother had fled a besieged Paris in 1871, now Proust made a similar departure for Cabourg once he was satisfied that his brother's wife and child were translated safely to Pau (Robert himself had been mobilized in August). The Battle of the Marne ensued and 250,000 French lives were lost. The capital, however, was saved and by December the government was back in Paris, directing the war effort. Proust returned from his last ever trip to Cabourg in October, his health disastrous but his resolve firm: his duty now was to finish what he had started with *Swann's Way*. The publication of the subsequent volumes would have to wait, though: during the conflict, as William Carter poignantly notes, 'because men and lead were needed for meaner tasks than typesetting books, Grasset and other publishers ceased operations'.[1]

Agostinelli's death robbed Proust of a companion; and mobilization deprived him of family, friends and attendants. Although not a French national, Reynaldo signed up and Fénelon, though he could have continued in his diplomatic posting, also volunteered for active service. With Nicolas Cottin and Odilon Albaret both promptly mobilized, Proust was soon without a valet and a driver. He recognized, though, the greater gravity of the situation: his own interests, he remarked in a letter of August 1914, 'seem quite stripped of importance when I think that millions of men are going to be massacred in a *War of the Worlds* comparable to that of Wells' (*Corr.*, XIII, 283). And in the years ahead he would lose many close friends.

If he was going to do his 'duty' to his work in Cabourg, he would need assistance. To this end he hired a handsome young Swede, Ernest Forssgren (1894–1970), who accompanied him and Céleste to the Normandy coast on 3 September 1914. When visiting Venice with his mother many years before he had travelled with Ruskin's heavy volumes: now his own manuscripts filled a whole suitcase that made the journey with them. Forssgren's role, however, was not merely practical. As Tadié puts it, 'the presence of this Nordic Adonis helped Marcel to detach himself from the image of another secretary who also used to play chequers by Proust's bed.'[2] Forssgren filled the gap left by Agostinelli but he and Céleste did not see eye to eye: Proust's housekeeper found the new arrival arrogant and full of ideas above his station, a perspective that is easily understood by readers of Forssgren's memoirs.[3] The Swede parted company with Proust shortly after their return from Cabourg, emigrating to New York to avoid conscription. Another man, a Swiss named Henri Rochat, would come to live in close proximity with Proust for a time in the last years of the latter's life, much to the detriment of his well-being. But these relations aside, from now on he would have three primary preoccupations, all of them in a perpetual tangle: his state of health, the developments of the war, and the progression of his still-evolving novel.

Proust followed the unfolding of the conflict obsessively. He read as many as seven newspapers each day (*Corr.*, xiv, 76) and was kept abreast of developments via his correspondence and visits from friends and acquaintances home on leave, who brought news from the Front to boulevard Haussmann. Proust was constantly concerned about being conscripted (despite being quite obviously unfit for service) and about being thought of as a shirker. He was alert to the commitment of all who served their country but he found the unthinking nationalistic prejudice of much of the contemporary newspaper coverage hard to palate. He disliked the blinkered jingoism of much contemporary discussion, the use of terms such as 'Boche'. He conceded, though, that such expressions, and the attitudes they reflect, 'are things that we can easily tolerate, so much do we suffer from thinking of the martyrdom of the soldiers and the officers and so moved are we by their sacrifice'; but he does condemn the widespread denigration of all things German (*Corr.*, xiii, 333). In the novel Proust's narrator argues, against the current of thought typified by the wartime writings of Maurice Barrès, that art worthy of the name *cannot* set out to be nationalistic, since the true artist is autonomous, his or her work embodying a unique, sovereign vision of the world. Proust's preferred wartime commentator was Henri Bidou in the *Journal des débats* and his least favourite articles were the 'Commentaires de Polybe' by Joseph Reinach in *Le Figaro*. The opinion pieces Proust read enrich and enliven the pages of his fiction: the unthinking Cottard, for example, parrots Germanophobic sentiments of the sort bemoaned by Proust, and Brichot's column, a favourite talking point of the Verdurins, bears a strong resemblance to Reinach's 'Commentaires'.[4] Pro-German opinions, magnified with dramatic and comic effect, are aired by the blustering Baron de Charlus during his night-time stroll with the narrator in *Time Regained*.

The year 1915 was one of uncertainty, anxiety and loss. Gaston de Caillavet died in early January, not a casualty of war but after a protracted illness. More bad news followed soon after: Proust's close friend Bertrand de Fénelon had been reported missing in December 1914 and a letter from his sister to Proust on 17 February intimated eyewitness corroboration of the rumour that Fénelon had gone down injured, possibly fatally, on the field of battle. Proust was unwilling to accept this; hopes and fear about Bertrand's state tormented him well into the spring, as did concerns for Reynaldo and Robert, Proust's brother. The war, as he put it, was his 'perpetual anxiety' (*Corr.*, XIV, 66). Finally Bibesco brought Proust word of Fénelon's death leading an advance, a scenario with which the death of Robert de Saint-Loup in the novel has much in common. Proust, whose precarious health had long made him certain of being survived by his acquaintances, was now being forced to come to terms with the iniquities of war and mortality. Fénelon's courage was 'all the more sublime for being quite pure of all hatred'; here was a hero whose patriotism was 'neither exclusive nor narrow' (*Corr.*, XIV, 71).[5] On 13 March *Le Figaro* confirmed all his worst fears: Fénelon's body had been recovered, identified by the photographs of his family that were found in his uniform; he had received a bullet in the head.

Proust's head, by his own admission clouded by his persistent use of the barbiturate Veronal to help him sleep, struggled to cope with this news. To add to his anxieties, in early April he was terrorized by a message convoking him to a military medical examination. The time of his appointment at the Hôtel de Ville was given as 3.30 a.m. (surely an error, but one that oddly suited his nocturnal regime); a note ominously indicated that non-attendance would be taken as the expression of availability for service. Proust's physician Dr Bize provided him with an unequivocal medical certificate (citing violent, daily asthma attacks, emphysema, kidney problems and heart trouble) in order to excuse him from this trial, but rather than an exemption Proust simply received a second convocation for an appointment later the same day. The certificate seemed to clear him of this second appointment, but he was contacted once more in late April, again at the end of June, then finally in August he received a visit from army doctors in his apartment at boulevard Haussmann. Abnormal sounds detected in his lungs were cause to adjourn any decision for six months. Sure that active service would kill him in one way or another, Proust was relieved, but his fears remained.

Céleste, acting now as secretary, messenger, *femme de chambre*, valet, nurse and cook (this latter only sporadically, for Proust's consumption of solids was largely limited to croissants taken with his coffee), experienced her own share of loss at this time. In April her mother died and very soon afterwards her brother was reported missing, possibly taken prisoner or killed in the Meuse. It fell to Proust to pass on this news, which he did directly but with tact and sensitivity. The letter he wrote to Marcelle Larivière, the daughter of Céleste's sister-in-law, in which he makes suggestions as to how Céleste might be looked after in her double grief back in Auxillac, is moving in its candour and quasi-parental tenderness. Proust (and the novel he produced) was marked by a number of short-lived loves for various artistic, aristocratic and otherwise alluring men – Jacques Bizet, Lucien Daudet, Fénelon, Agostinelli – but besides his mother, the person who perhaps understood him best, who most attracted his affectionate admiration and to whom he was most devoted, was an uneducated housekeeper.

Progress with the novel was slow. His asthma meant that Proust performed his 'fumigations' with the Legras powders for up to six hours at a stretch, after which he would attempt to work on his novel. Repeatedly he turned down social invitations, refused to make plans and was extremely reluctant even to receive visits in his bearded, weakened state. Work being carried out on a neighbouring property began at just the time that Proust was falling asleep (around 7.30 a.m.), so he found himself '[forced] to take terrible and useless doses of narcotics' (*Corr.*, XIV, 199). As he struggled with his own physical plight in Paris, at the Front his younger brother was sleeping under canvas, operating on wounded servicemen, often through the night, in extremely dangerous conditions and had contracted dysentery. Proust's circumstances were far removed from the horrors that confronted Robert, but the brothers were connected by the same bloody-minded determination to persevere in their chosen vocation. 'I know I would be useless in the army,' wrote Proust to Lionel Hauser in August 1915, 'but I yearn to finish the work I've started and to set down in it truths that I know will nourish many others and which, if I don't do this, will die with me' (*Corr.*, XIV, 212–13).

Proust's correspondence with Hauser, his financial adviser, grew increasingly frequent from October 1915 and continued steadily through the next two years. This was due to Proust's inability to manage his money, coupled with his spirited but often misguided will to speculate on the markets. His position had been complicated by the collapse in value of shares he held; and by the suspension and subsequent liquidation of the stock exchange, together with the strictures for investors that this brought. Overdue payments on loans were mounting up at eye-watering interest rates, he had funds in a number of different banks and drew on the services of a number of different brokers. His affairs were in a disastrous state: Hauser's forbearance and calm were quite extraordinary but at times the thinness of his patience shows through: 'there are people who are born for this métier, and others who are born to have their fingers burned trying', wrote Hauser on 26 October, continuing: 'I don't think I exaggerate when I say that you belong to the latter category, but if you are not convinced of this, you are free to carry on with the experiment, I ask only to be convinced of the contrary' (*Corr.*, XIV, 255). Through a combination of good fortune and adhering more or less to Hauser's successive plans to re-establish an equilibrium in his finances, Proust managed to remain afloat through these years, although pecuniary concerns underpin a long chain of correspondence with Mme Catusse and others in late 1917 and 1918, regarding the sale of various pieces of furniture and other household effects (proceeds from which, showing characteristic generosity, he intended to share with Mme Scheikévitch, a friend in financial trouble brought about by the revolution in her native Russia).

When the military medics came to examine Proust in August, they offended him by mistaking him for an architect and not recognizing the name of the revered medical family to which he belonged (*Corr.*, XIV, 228). Their taking Proust for an architect, though, is not as off beam as it may at first seem. The multi-layered complexity of the design and construction of his novel is of a sort to compete with that of the grandest of building projects; indeed, Proust's fascination with cathedrals, fostered through his reading of Ruskin and Emile Mâle, led him, for a time, to contemplate naming the sections of his novel after various components of cathedral architecture.[6] In a letter to Antoine Bibesco Proust attests to multiplicity in even the smallest details of his design, citing aspects of sonatas by Saint-Saëns and Franck, the prelude to Wagner's *Lohengrin* and a 'Ballade' by Fauré as all contributing to Vinteuil's sonata and its 'little phrase' (*Corr.*, XIV, 234–6). The complexity of the novel's overarching structure was also emerging: *Swann* had appeared; proofs of the first version of *The Guermantes Way* had been printed for Grasset in June 1914; appetites had been whetted by extracts from that volume and what would become *Within a Budding Grove*, published in the June and July 1914 numbers of the *NRF*; the material for the close of *Time Regained* was in place (although the volume was expanding as Proust added to the section dealing with the war that was being waged as he wrote). And now, from its centre, the novel was growing yet further.

Mme Scheikévitch, of whom Proust was fond, had lost her brother in battle. Proust borrowed her copy of *Swann's Way* so as to inscribe for her, in the blank pages at the front, 'an episode quite different from the rest and the only one which can at present find in your wounded heart affinities with your pain' (*Corr.*, XIV, 273). From Proust's lengthy inscription we can gain a sense of the novel's development in late 1915. After the fashion of the prepublication pieces that appeared in 1913 in *Le Figaro*, the pages he wrote for Mme Scheikévitch are a patchwork of quotation from the *cahiers* that make up *Sodom and Gomorrah* and, above all, *The Captive* and *The Fugitive*. He summarizes the central narrative lines of the Albertine cycle, sometimes glossing, sometimes quoting material that readers of the finished novel will recognize. Already in November 1915, less than eighteen months after Agostinelli's death, Proust had channelled his emotional upheaval into a fiction, the creation of which had allowed him to come to terms with – or at least better understand – his loss. The letter quoted above, explaining to Mme Scheikévitch his motivations for sharing with her this tale of loss, allows us to appreciate the cathartic power of the creative process for Proust.

His creative efforts in 1915 to 1916 were directed towards the development of *Sodom and Gomorrah*, the central volume of the novel in which homosexuality – and in particular 'sexual inversion', to use the lexis of the time – is most fully explored. 'Without any immoral intent, I must tell you,' wrote Proust of this volume the following summer to Gallimard, 'its portraiture is of the most complete and audacious veracity' (*Corr.*, XV, 130). Finally in the pages of his work Proust was able to explore issues he had observed, confronted and lived through relatively privately for many years; he was able, indeed, to revisit in a sustained manner questions raised more fleetingly in early stories (such as 'Before Night') and in the scene of voyeurism at Montjouvain in 'Combray'. *Sodom and Gomorrah* is a bridge, a sequence of revelations leading from the early social and personal development of the narrator to the mature travails of the Albertine cycle.

Much to Proust's delight, Reynaldo returned on leave in the autumn and Proust managed to attend an evening party at which his friend, together with pianist Edouard Hermann, played his new waltzes for two pianos, composed in the field and dedicated to his fellow servicemen. Proust, admiring, enraptured and still unsure whether his own work of art would reach an audience and live on beyond his death, wrote to Reynaldo: 'how happy you must be . . . to have incarnated yourself in these immortal forms and how you mustn't give a damn about any worries after this! How I envy you!' (*Corr.*, XIV, 289–90). Proust grew closer to a friend of Hahn's, Henri Bardac, during 1915: he had been relieved from active service after being seriously injured in the Battle of the Marne, but went on to serve as an attaché in the French embassy in London and would see Proust during his regular trips back to Paris. His lover was a valet named Charlie Humphries, whose name is echoed in that of Charlie Morel, the valet's son who becomes the lover of the Baron de Charlus, the libidinal trajectory of whom is so central to *Sodom and Gomorrah*. Another attaché Proust got to know was Paul Morand (1888–1976), a diplomat and writer who knew Bardac and had met Fénelon at the embassy in London. Morand and Bardac shared an admiration for *Swann's Way* and Proust and Morand soon became correspondents and friends, dining regularly together at the Ritz in the company of Princesse Hélène Soutzo, who would later become Morand's wife.

These sparkling associates were not Proust's only social connections of the time. The darker side of Sodom fascinated Proust and drew him into locales rather less salubrious than the private dining rooms of the Ritz. During the war Albert le Cuziat, who had previously served as head footman to Prince Alexis Orloff, who had also employed Ernest Forssgren, is known to have run a bath house for men near the Madeleine church; he then opened a male brothel, the Hôtel Marigny in the rue de l'Arcade, not far from boulevard Haussmann. Le Cuziat was for Proust an important source of gossip, scandal and anecdote about the goings on behind the closed doors of his establishment, which accommodated men from all levels of society. Olivier Dabescat, the restaurant manager at the Ritz, played a similar role for Proust who gave both men ample tips in return for their intelligence. There is no doubt that Proust frequented Le Cuziat's establishment;[7] but there are competing versions of what he did there. Céleste Albaret explains that he was quite candid about his trips to the Hôtel Marigny, giving her a rundown on his return of whom and what he had seen. She insists that his trips were fact-finding missions made in order to observe the goings-on of the world so as better to write about them. On one occasion, for a fee, Le Cuziat allowed him, hidden in an adjoining room, to witness 'a big industrialist who makes the journey especially from the North of France' who is 'attached to a wall with chains and padlocks, while a real wretch, picked up who knows where and paid for the privilege, whips him until blood spurts all over the place. And it is only then that the unfortunate individual reaches the climax of his pleasures.' Céleste could not believe that such a thing could take place; Proust insisted that he did not invent it, and when Céleste asked 'but how could you watch it?' his response, according to Albaret, was simple: 'Precisely because you couldn't make it up.'[8] As readers of *Time Regained* are aware, this scene is directly transplanted into Proust's fiction, taking place in a brothel run by Jupien in wartime Paris, where the masochistic recipient of the blows is not a prominent industrialist but the aristocratic Baron de Charlus.

Céleste is at pains in her memoirs to refute stories that had circulated about Proust's other reputed activities, stemming from the account of a man who had worked as a prostitute for Le Cuziat, which was found recorded in a notebook of the novelist Marcel Jouhandeau and repeated by George Painter among others. The man described how Proust would pay to watch young men masturbate while following suit himself beneath a bed sheet pulled up to his chin. The man claimed that if Proust was unable to achieve orgasm this way, then Le Cuziat would bring in cages containing starved rats which were set upon each other: the sight of the ensuing tooth and claw struggle stimulated Proust and allowed him to achieve his pleasure.[9] Céleste flatly denies the possibility of Proust having anything other than platonic relations with anyone (her book often verges into hero worship). She disputes this particular story on the grounds of Proust's documented aversion to rats and mice; but the image of Proust lying in bed, quite out of reach of the other man, tallies with his increasing fear of germs and contamination in his last years and the tendency, which surfaces in his writing, to privilege observation over (inter)action. We will never know for sure how or with whom Proust found his pleasure but such details are little more than titillation for the prurient. Whatever our preferences or tastes, if we are interested in the pursuit of pleasure, its risks and its rewards, there are few better studies than *In Search of Lost Time*.

New Year, in Proust's eyes, was always difficult: a symbolic moment when we are tempted to entertain brave expectations, to hope for new beginnings, yet one which, with increasing frequency as we get older, tends to confront us with the painful truth that nothing has changed – only time has passed and death is a little nearer. In *Within a Budding Grove* the narrator experiences this for the first time when he realizes that the much anticipated new year will in fact bring no necessary change in his relation with Gilberte. And this same dismal sensation, the recognition in the new year of the crushing yet beautifully cadenced '*matière éternelle et commune, l'humidité familière, l'ignorante fluidité des anciens jours*' (the eternal common substance, the familiar moisture, the unheeding fluidity of the old days'; *Budding Grove*, 69; I, 479), was felt acutely by Proust in 1916: 'Alas', he wrote to Antoine Bibesco, 'there will be violets, apple blossom, before those there will be blooms of frost, but no more will there be Bertrand' (*Corr.*, xv, 23).

The deaths of friends and the absence of others close to him saddened Proust, yet he maintained a hard streak of realism: 'I am only myself when I am alone', he wrote starkly in 1916, 'and I only profit from others in so far as they permit me discoveries within myself' (*Corr.*, xv, 27). Proust's work was everything and solitude was a necessary condition for it. As the narrator explains at the end of *A la recherche*, 'real books should be the offspring not of daylight and casual talk but of darkness and silence' (*Time Regained*, 257; iv, 476). In these conditions (what he described as 'the absurd life that I lead'; *Corr.*, xv, 27), his eyesight was diminishing and caused him great troubles throughout 1916 and 1917, which could have been rectified but for his refusal to disrupt his routine with a daytime visit to an optician. Still, undeterred, via his correspondence his search for details continued: early in 1916 he borrowed essay plans from Céleste's niece while revising a passage of *Within a Budding Grove* where the girls discuss an assignment that one of their number, Gisèle, was set for her *certificat d'études*. Around the same time he posed a succession of ever more detailed questions to Reynaldo's sister, Maria de Madrazo, about the working practice of the celebrated dressmaker Fortuny (the nephew of Maria's husband). Fortuny, born in Spain the same year as Proust but now based in Venice, made dresses famous for the beauty and intricacy of their fabrics. Proust wanted to know if certain motifs featured in his dresses and whether particular paintings in Venice might have inspired him. He explained to Maria that his narrator gives Albertine a Fortuny dress which, when he tires of her, evokes the allure of Venice and increases his will to leave her; after her flight, when the narrator visits Venice, seeing a painting by Carpaccio (Proust has not yet decided which one at this stage – in the final version it is the *Miracle of the Relic of the True Cross at the Rialto Bridge*, a painting Proust refers to as the *Patriarch of Grado*) triggers an involuntary memory of Albertine and renders Venice sorrowful. This detail, 'the Fortuny "leitmotif"' as he calls it, will play a role that 'is by turns sensual, poetic and sorrowful' (*Corr.*, xv, 57).

Exchanges such as this reveal the labours behind the slightest of details in *A la recherche*. But Proust's mind had much more to focus on besides the intricacies of the motifs on his grand fresco: in February he received a visit from André Gide who wished to talk once more about transferring publication of the novel to the NRF. Proust had not received any royalties from Grasset for almost a year and the intellectual reputation of Gide, Gallimard and others still exerted a powerful pull. But changing publisher was risky: if the NRF took him on but then changed their minds and dropped him before all the volumes had appeared (and even Proust could see that this would take time), then the essential lifeline would be cut – his novel would die with him. If he was going to move his novel to the NRF, Gallimard would have to convince Proust of a commitment to the whole work, come what may. After Gide's visit, Proust corresponded with Gallimard, the latter offering various assurances in response to Proust's previously voiced concerns about the 'indecency' of the work, the undesirability of its great length and so on.[10] Proust's wish, quite simply, was to assure 'the safeguarding . . . in a book that will maybe outlive me, of all that I have most intimately thought and felt' (*Corr.*, xv, 131). Grasset, who was convalescing in Switzerland after typhoid fever had ended his active service, felt let down but responded much as he had when the NRF made overtures to Proust in early 1914: he had no wish to restrict the freedom of an author who had lost confidence in him. This time for Proust, pragmatism and ambition won out over his sentiments for a friend and associate – he sided with the future of his work – and in September 1916 the deal was struck: the remaining volumes (and a re-edition of *Swann*) would be published by the NRF.

Coincidentally or otherwise, during these months of negotiation, when almost every letter Proust wrote made mention of his debilitating eye pain ('I'm in the process of losing my sight', he claimed in May; *Corr.*, xv, 105), music appears progressively to have grown in importance for the author. In March 1916, just a few months after delighting in Hahn's waltzes, he wrote that Beethoven's late quartets and the music of Franck had been 'for some years . . . [his] principal spiritual nourishment' (*Corr.*, xv, 61). The writing on music we encounter in *A la recherche* has an extraordinary beauty and suggestive power. Such writing was founded on exceptionally focused acts of listening, intense, repeated submersions in particular pieces of music.[11] Proust would hear music performed via the Théâtrophone until he cancelled his telephone line in December 1914 and, when he was able to go out, at concerts or receptions, but his poor health and the social distractions of such receptions made them unreliable sources of the nourishment he dearly cherished. His solution was to invite musicians to play for him at home, where he listened serenely, recumbent, his eyes shut. Gaston Poulet's ensemble played Beethoven's Thirteenth Quartet and Franck's Quartet for Proust at boulevard Haussmann in April 1916. A second performance included a repeat of the Franck and the addition of Fauré's Piano Quartet. When the ensemble reached the end of the Franck quartet, Proust's dark eyes opened and he asked them to play the piece over from the start. Signs of reluctance from the tired foursome (it was at least 2 a.m.) were dissipated by the extravagant payment he handed to each of them. In her memoirs Céleste recalls only one private performance and she places it in 1920, but this is plainly contradicted by Proust's letters, which attest to at least two performances in 1916, and by Massis, the viola player, who suggests there were many.[12] In points of detail the accounts diverge: did Proust collect the musicians in a taxi, wrapped in an eiderdown and bearing a bowl of mashed potatoes? Was it champagne or cider that was served in the apartment, with or without chips? It matters little. At bottom what these episodes from Proust's odd existence reveal is how far he was willing to go for experiences of pleasure that were intense and intimate. Whether it was a rent boy or a string quartet at the foot of his bed, Proust, it seems, wished to witness every movement, every step towards satisfaction, every note that contributes to the composer's creation.

To see him at such moments, suggested Céleste, was to see him 'transfigured and illuminated from within'.[13] Such illumination and exhilaration are transferred in turn to Proust's readers each time we read his pages on desire, or on the narrator's experience of first hearing Vinteuil's septet in *The Captive*, pages enriched by these intimate concerts at the boulevard Haussmann.

The highs of these contemplative moments were interspersed, of course, with the lows brought about by the fragility of Proust's health: a stretch of 70 hours of insomnia in May, heart palpitations in August and persistent eye pain. But somehow he worked through these trials and in November 1916 was able to deliver the completed manuscript of *Within a Budding Grove* to Gallimard, together with the first twenty pages of the proofs of *The Guermantes Way* that he had received from Grasset in 1914. He explained that he had his whole novel now in manuscript form; as he received his proofs from the printers he would start to send them back the subsequent volumes, two manuscript notebooks at a time. The NRF's printer had difficulties in keeping to this regime, however, so Proust's plan was eventually abandoned. For the time being, though, there was major progress: his work was back en route to publication.

Buoyed up, perhaps, by a new confidence about the future of his work, Proust was more active in 1917, accepting more visitors and making more trips out, particularly to the theatre and to dinners at the Ritz. But this is not to say that his attention had strayed from the war. The conflict continued and Proust, in a New Year letter to his old friend Mme Straus, stated that as long as the Germans remained so close, 'it [was] not easy to have happiness nor even to dare to hope for it' (*Corr.*, XVI, 32). Paul Morand visited Proust at boulevard Haussmann in February and described the bloodless pallor of his bearded host, wrapped up in ragged woollens charred, as Albaret confirms, from being repeatedly warmed for him in the oven.[14] The room was cold (Proust felt central heating aggravated his asthma) but the conversation was warm and lively. Another relation of friendship and mutual admiration that Proust developed at this time was with Walter Berry, an American lawyer who had been a judge at the International Tribunal in Cairo before moving to France, where he became President of the American Chamber of Commerce in Paris in late 1916. They became acquainted when Berry sent Proust a volume dating from 1709 that he had found in a bookseller's, which bore the coat of arms of the now defunct Guermantes family. A friend of Edith Wharton and Henry James, Berry was a fluent French speaker and well connected, playing an important diplomatic role in wartime Paris and increasingly so after the U.S. joined the war in April 1917. He was made an officer in the Légion d'Honneur in September 1918, an event that a delighted Proust described as 'a New Year's day for me, at an age when I no longer have them' (*Corr.*, XVII, 371).

Proust may have been attending dinners but this did not mean he was dining: he would take champagne and drink vast quantities of coffee but seldom ate anything. Indeed, in March 1917 he reported that he weighed only 45 kilograms (just over 7 stone). The same month he had flu that aggravated his asthma, causing a cough that was somewhere between a spasmodic bark and a continual groan, such that he was convinced that his neighbours would think he had bought a church organ, or a dog, or fathered a child that was suffering from whooping cough (*Corr.*, XVI, 86). He may have lost his breath, but not his sense of humour. Beyond his own ailments, the well-being of his brother was still a concern: in April 1917 he confided anxiously to Clément de Maugny that he had received only four or five letters from Robert since the start of the war (*Corr.*, XVI, 107). It was a relief, then, to see him back in Paris on leave at the end of the month, although Proust was concerned by his brother's rather run-down state. The commitment and devotion to medicine their father had shown to the very end of his life was plain for all to see in Robert, now Commandant Proust.

Proust's spirits were raised by the request that came in April from Jacques-Emile Blanche, the painter of his portrait a quarter of a century earlier, to be the dedicatee of a collection of his essays on artists. Proust was only too happy to oblige when the painter also asked him to write a preface for the book (it was eventually published in March 1919 as *Propos de peintre: De David à Degas*). As Proust reread Blanche's writings on the recent greats – Manet, Whistler and others – in preparation for his preface, while international conflict continued to rage on the battlefields, a collaboration of some of the world's most exciting practitioners of contemporary art was unfolding on the stage of the Théâtre du Châtelet. In May Jean Cocteau's ballet *Parade* was first performed by the Ballets Russes, with music by Erik Satie (including the sound of typewriters and boats' whistles), choreography by the great Léonide Massine, with decor and costumes by Picasso (on whose handsomeness Proust commented to Cocteau). The programme note written by Guillaume Apollinaire featured the first use of the term *surréalisme*, an anticipation of one of the twentieth century's most important artistic movements. Avant-garde artistic modernity flashed across the stage and crashed from the orchestra pit. Proust praised it in a letter to Cocteau (although he was left nonplussed by Stravinsky's *Petrouchka*, which followed on the bill), but neither critics nor public were so appreciative and the ballet's run was cut short. *Parade* did not have an immediate success, but as Proust put it in *Within a Budding Grove*, sometimes years, 'centuries even . . . must elapse before the public can begin to cherish a masterpiece that is really new' (*Budding Grove*, 120; I, 522). His health, his idiosyncratic way of working, the mammoth nature of his undertaking – all these factors held back Proust's novel: Cocteau and others were younger, bolder and faster moving. The more immediate, sudden impact of music, dance, poetry and visual art naturally commanded attention and announced the arrival of an avant-garde, but Proust's work, as time would show, also shook orthodoxies and challenged preconceptions; it just took longer to materialize.

His moment was soon to come but first he faced a battle: 'I've received 5,000 pages of proofs to correct', he wrote to Mme Catusse in October 1917 when the *NRF*'s printers delivered the first instalment of *Within a Budding Grove*, 'which will make 15,000 since I'll have to correct them three times over, without spectacles and with very little eyesight' (*Corr.*, XVI, 257). As so often with Proust, the numbers were exaggerated; but the task was undoubtedly a daunting one. He had not received proofs for the whole volume, however, and towards the end of the year a lack of staff meant that printing stopped altogether; Proust had to wait until April 1918 for the proofs to start arriving again and even then there were gaps and problems. In June he returned his corrected proofs of *Within a Budding Grove* and submitted the complete manuscript of *The Guermantes Way* to the printers, but was still awaiting the proofs for that volume in October. Gallimard ultimately withdrew the manuscript and sent it to another printer, together with the materials for the other volumes that were ready for printing. Having despaired for months about a lack of proofs, at one stroke Proust was submerged, just under a month after Armistice Day in December 1918, receiving page proofs for 'four volumes to correct all at once' (*Corr.*, XVII, 502), among them *Pastiches et mélanges*, a collection of Proust's journalistic writings that Gallimard had also agreed to publish and that Proust had assembled in the spring, including a new pastiche of Saint-Simon.[15] Ten years before, just as his novel was taking shape, Proust had quoted the Gospel of John, via Ruskin: 'Work while you still have light.' Now there was more work than ever to do, and the concerns Proust had long been voicing about the fading of his light seemed somewhat more urgent.

The bombardment of Paris meant that life for those who remained in the capital was perilous. Proust had observed an air raid from a balcony of the Ritz hotel in late July 1917, a scene that

Jean Cocteau's vision of the adult Proust wrapped up against the cold, 1920.

he perceived as one of great beauty; his letter depicting the planes 'climbing and descending . . . making or unmaking the constellations' (*Corr.*, XVI, 196) is textually very close to the description of a raid found in *Time Regained*. In January 1918 a taxi taking the author home from a performance of Borodin's Second String Quartet broke down during the first raid on Paris by Germany's Gotha heavy bombers. The impatient Proust walked the short distance home from the avenue de Messine as bombs landed just a few hundred metres away in the rue d'Athènes. In June Céleste found fragments of shrapnel in the brim of his hat after he had walked home during another raid. The fragile aesthete seemed still to have the steely core that saw him through his duel with Jean Lorrain two decades earlier. Throughout the war Proust was the only inhabitant of his building not to take shelter in the cellar when the sirens sounded. His asthma and sensitivity to the cold meant that he stayed put in his bedroom.

Rather than fearing the Gothas or the long-range 'Paris Gun' siege artillery that started bombarding the capital in March, Proust worried that such threats might cause Céleste to retreat to her provincial home town, leaving him alone. Proust had never made a bed in his life: when faced, as an overnight guest during his military service, with a bed and a set of blankets and sheets, he got tangled up in the latter and ended up sleeping on the bare mattress.[16] Fending for himself, it seems, was never really an option.

Beside the dangers and risks of wartime life, Proust's body was showing new signs of frailty: he was having problems with his memory and to a number of correspondents in March and April 1918 he explained that he was feeling ill in a new way that he did not wish to disclose. Fearing that he was suffering from the onset of facial paralysis and aphasia, the loss of the ability to speak, which his mother had suffered shortly before her death, in June he consulted Dr Babinsky, a neurologist and pupil, like Sigmund Freud, of the great Jean-Martin Charcot. The specialist reassured Proust, who (never one for half-measures) had thought his ills might be cured by trepanation, the drilling of holes in the skull. Fortunately such measures were not required. A likely source of Proust's symptoms was poisoning resulting from his ongoing and increasing use of Veronal and caffeine to counter his insomnia and fatigue. He may have attempted to moderate his use of these but such endeavours seem never to have lasted long: by December 1918 Proust was casually mentioning to Lionel Hauser his habit of taking six cups of coffee after dinner (*Corr.*, xvii, 501).

In April Jacques de Lacretelle, a man of letters of Proust's acquaintance, sent him a rare edition of *Swann's Way* requesting that the author autograph it. Proust did rather more: like the inscription to Mme Scheikévitch that outlined the Albertine narrative, Proust filled the first three pages of Lacretelle's book with a dedication that sheds a good deal of light on the question of the 'keys' to the people and places of that volume. 'There are no keys for the characters in this book,' he wrote, 'or rather there are eight or ten for each one' (*Corr.*, XVII, 193). Various churches and cathedrals (Lisieux, Evreux, the Sainte-Chapelle) underpin different aspects of the Combray church; many phrases and melodies lie behind Vinteuil's imaginary compositions in the novel. And the same, *mutatis mutandis*, goes for the monocles so wittily described at the 'soirée Sainte-Euverte'. 'I repeat,' concluded Proust categorically, 'the characters are entirely invented and there is no single key' (*Corr.*, XVII, 194).

Readers of *A la recherche* have always been tempted to seek out keys for Proust's characters. The key to Albertine, the love (and despair) of the narrator's life, is most commonly thought to be Alfred Agostinelli. Another man, however, entered Proust's life during 1918 and undoubtedly played a role in the development of the Albertine cycle, but the more obvious parallels between Agostinelli and Albertine have meant that Henri Rochat is a rather less familiar figure. Rochat worked at the Ritz, a Swiss waiter who became a friend, a source of gossip and soon came to live with Proust in an arrangement not unlike that of the narrator and Albertine, although Rochat served intermittently, for a time, as Proust's secretary.[17] Rochat was a drain on his emotional and financial resources who, in William Carter's words, 'attached himself to Proust with all the tenacity of a barnacle on a rock'.[18] During the time they were together Proust wrote of his 'heartache', which had brought with it 'considerable financial difficulties' (*Corr.*, XVII, 360, 367). 'I have embarked on sentimental dealings', he confided to Mme Straus in October 1918, 'from which there is no way out, no joy, and which create a perpetual stream of fatigue, suffering and absurd expenditure' (*Corr.*, XVII, 483). Proust bought Rochat clothes and gifts; the waiter had a taste for jewels, which Proust satisfied; he also had a taste for women (he was engaged), which caused tension between the men. Like Albertine, his hobby was drawing and painting. By the summer of 1919 Proust

Manuscript page of *Sodom and Gomorrah*.

454

sought the documents necessary for Rochat to return safely to Switzerland; while awaiting the papers, however, Rochat went to the Côte d'Azur, spent a great deal of Proust's money and returned with a venereal infection. Proust accompanied Rochat to the Gare de Lyon in early July 1919, clearly keen to make a clean break and to assure the young man's departure. Unable to find work, Rochat, boomerang-like, was back before the end of the month and rein- stalled in Proust's apartment, a situation which now, as Proust put it, 'poisoned [his] existence' (*Corr.*, XVIII, 355). Ultimately, through the good offices of an old friend, Horace Finaly, Proust found Rochat a position in a bank in Buenos Aires and somehow persuaded him to board a ship for Argentina, but this was not until June 1921.

Just as the publication of *Swann's Way* was darkened by Agostin- elli's disappearance from Paris in late 1913, so the major events of Proust's last years – the resumption of the publication of his novel and the public recognition of its brilliance – took place against a private backdrop of tension, anxiety and discontent, the tortuousness of which the narrator's words in *The Captive* surely come close to encapsulating: 'we lived a day-to-day life which, however tedious, was still endurable, held down to earth by the ballast of habit and by that certainty that the next day, even if it should prove painful, would contain the presence of the other' (*The Captive*, 404; III, 856).

In November 1918, when the armistice came, Proust wrote sombrely to Mme Straus: 'Together we have thought too much about the war not to share a tender word on the night of victory, joyous because of this, melancholic because of those we loved who will not see it' (*Corr.*, XVII, 448). Five years had passed since the publication of *Swann's Way* and the world had changed immeasurably in this time. In re-editing the 1913 Grasset edition of *Swann's Way* for re-release under the NRF imprint in 1919, Proust's most significant change was to the fictional geography of the novel. In the revised text that we read today, Combray is no longer in its original location near Chartres, southwest of Paris, but near Laon, to the northwest of the capital. In making this change, Proust placed the village squarely in the path of the advancing German army and was able to incorporate the fictional 'battle of Méséglise' into his narrative of the war in *Time Regained*. The war did not simply provide Proust with the time to expand a fiction that was planned out in his mind; it became a part of the evolving fabric of that fiction and shaped it in ways the author could never have foreseen when he began to fill the pages of his *carnet* in 1908.

Proust's wish was that his remaining volumes should appear together at once, but the process of turning his manuscript into printed proofs and the corrected proofs into bound volumes was exceedingly slow and, by his calculations, could take until 1925 to complete. Were this so, he worried, 'readers will have long since forgotten the existence of Swann and the whole thing will be a failure' (*Corr.*, xvii, 442). He was almost right about the timescale – *Time Regained* was not published until 1927 – but the *Search* was no failure. Its final shape, though, was far from settled. Proust wrote a summary of his work in a 1918 printing of *Within a Budding Grove* in which he noted the subsequent volumes as being entitled *The Guermantes Way*, *Sodom and Gomorrah I* and *Sodom and Gomorrah II: Time Regained*, making five volumes in all.[19] According to the schematic sketches Proust provided of the key episodes in each volume, *Sodom and Gomorrah I* corresponds largely to what we know as *Sodom and Gomorrah*; the Albertine cycle material, however, did not yet exist in discrete, named volumes, but rather as the first part of *Sodom and Gomorrah II: Time Regained*. The final volume divisions and the titles as we know them would not be finalized until 1922. A great deal remained to be done, but after suffering from bronchitis in December 1918, the next phase of Proust's great task of correcting proofs and finalizing his manuscript coincided in January with a bout of laryngitis, a persistent high fever and then disastrous news: 102 boulevard Haussmann had been sold and Proust, at this vital moment, would have to find a new home.

8

# Recognition and Decline

I sacrifice to this work my pleasures, my health, my life.
Letter to Jean de Pierrefeu, January 1920

Moving house did not represent simply the prospect of disruption
and inconvenience. It brought for Proust a very real fear of renewed
financial difficulties. He had amassed a significant debt of unpaid
rent that would have to be paid on his departure. Even if he
managed to pay, where would he go? As so often in Proust's life,
his charm worked its wonders and a friend intervened on his
behalf: the Duc de Guiche cut a deal with the banker who had
bought 102 boulevard Haussmann and, remarkably, managed to
have the rent arrears waived, to have a payment equivalent to three
months' rent made to Proust as well as another, additional indemnity,
all on the simple proviso that the tenant vacate the apartment by
1 June 1919. This did not diminish the inevitable stress of the move
for Proust but it certainly went some way towards relieving his
immediate financial concerns.

Eventually accommodation was found courtesy of Jacques Porel,
the son of Réjane (1856–1920), the famous actress much admired
by Proust, whose traits are found in the fictional actress La Berma
in *A la recherche*. Réjane owned a small apartment at 8 bis rue
Laurent-Pichat, which was vacant; it fulfilled Proust's need for shelter
and basic comforts but it soon proved to be far from ideal for the
writer seeking respite from the weltering of the world. He repeatedly

complained about the 'walls of paper' in the block, which meant that he heard not only the declamations of the actor Le Bargy, who lived across the courtyard, but also the conversations – and the frequent, vocal, enthusiastic love-making – of his immediate neighbours. 'I'll never be able to correct proofs here', he wrote to Walter Berry less than a month after moving in; by July, with works going on that prevented him sleeping, his lodgings had become 'Hell', 'a martyrdom' (*Corr.*, xviii, 281; 290; 298). Although a great deal of work editing and finalizing the definitive shape of the novel remained to be done, towards the end of May, before moving to rue Laurent-Pichat, Proust wrote to Gallimard explaining that if the publication of his novel was not completed during his lifetime, he had 'left all [his] notebooks numbered' and would 'count on' Gallimard to complete the publication on the basis of this text (*Corr.*, xviii, 226). Given this, it is reasonable to assume that it was around this time that there took place the scene recounted by Céleste Albaret of Proust triumphantly informing her that he had at last written the word '*Fin*' (The End) at the close of *Time Regained*.[1] 'The important thing', he told Céleste, was that he would no longer be anxious: 'My work can appear. I won't have given my life for nothing.'[2] According to Céleste, towards the end of the war, she burned 32 *cahiers* at Proust's instruction, the school notebooks in which it is thought a primitive, by then superseded, version of the novel was contained. Although work on the continuity and overall coherence of the novel would occupy Proust until his death (and remain unfinished), this most irrevocable parting with early draft material suggests a good degree of confidence in the final shape of the novel by the summer of 1919.[3]

Proust's cork-lined bedroom at boulevard Haussmann has been reconstructed in the Musée Carnavalet in Paris using the original furniture: the old metal bedstead tarnished by the fumes from his Legras powders, a folding Chinese screen, a small rosewood side table. All these objects, along with the invaluable *cahiers* of

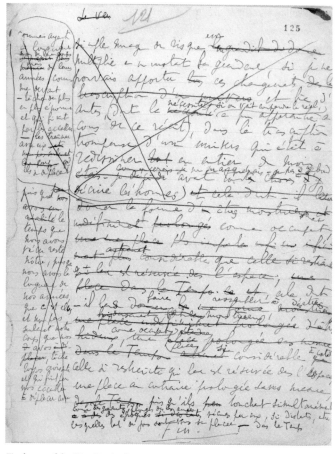

Final page of the *Time Regained* manuscript, *c.* 1919.

manuscript, many of them bulging with pasted-on additions, the
notebooks, the *paperoles* (loose-leaf jottings and scribblings), his
singed sweaters, his linen, his 'Sergeant Major' nibs and his ink,
his coffee and his medicines: all were packed and migrated from
the last home with links to his now long-departed parents to the
much more modest apartment on rue Laurent-Pichat. And life went

on: the following day, 1 June 1919, Proust was in print again: the first post-war number of the *NRF* included a piece extracted from *Within a Budding Grove*.

If the war had effaced readers' memories of *Swann's Way* and its author, then the *NRF* pages on the decline of the narrator's love for Gilberte were at once a reminder and an *amuse-bouche* for an impending feast, for just three weeks later, on 21 June, there appeared three volumes bearing Proust's name on their spines. The volume of collected occasional pieces, *Pastiches et mélanges* and the re-release of *Swann's Way* were the *hors d'œuvres*; the main dish was the long-delayed follow-up, *Within a Budding Grove*. This latter was not to everyone's tastes, however. The narrative of an adolescent's sexual and artistic awakenings, split between pre-war Paris and the leisured locales of the Normandy coast, differed markedly in tone, style and substance from recent celebrated works. The winners of the prestigious Goncourt Prize for the four years prior to 1919 had all been war novels by writers who had seen active service, books such as *Le Feu* (*Fire*, by Henri Barbusse, 1916) and *La Flamme au poing* (*The Flame that is France*, by Henry Malherbe, 1917) that celebrated the lives of soldiers and civilians affected by the war, books that contrasted all too starkly for some with what they took to be Proust's indulgent, delicate study of *jeunes filles en fleurs*. Some critics, though, were alert to the quality of the writing: Denys Amiel in *Le Pays*, for example, cast Proust as 'a memoire writer like Retz and Saint-Simon . . . a novelist like Balzac, Tolstoy, Dickens or the Zola of the *Rougon* [*Macquart*] – a historian like Michelet . . . a moralist like La Bruyère . . .' (*Corr.*, XVIII, 365, n. 2). Proust naturally was pleased with these comparisons but wrote to correct Amiel's view that his writing was unsystematic, its movements contingent, creating 'a vertiginous disorder'. Proust's perspective, which he underlined repeatedly in letters to critics and friends, was that his novel was intricately constructed 'in the architectural sense' and based upon 'principles of literary architecture' (*Corr.*, XVIII, 365; 389). For example he explained to François Mauriac, who had been shocked by the apparently gratuitous voyeuristic scene in *Swann's Way* where the narrator witnesses the erotic encounter between Mlle Vinteuil and her girlfriend at Montjouvain, that it was carefully built into that volume 'as an explanation of the jealousy of my young hero in the fourth and fifth volumes' (*Corr.*, XVIII, 404).

To his critics Proust's work may have seemed out of sync with its times but his open-minded and discerning appreciation of Cocteau's treatise on modern music, *Le Coq et l'harlequin*, in June 1919, and his principled rejection of reactionary literary-political dogmatism as embodied in the manifesto 'Pour un parti de l'intelligence', published the following month in *Le Figaro*'s literary supplement and signed by Daniel Halévy and other prominent intellectuals, are the responses of a critically engaged thinker alert to the issues of his times, not those of a blinkered, self-absorbed aesthete. The support of friends and acquaintances who recognized what he was seeking to achieve was important to him, which made the publication in October of Paul Morand's 'Ode to Marcel Proust' all the more hurtful. Morand's poem publically made fun of Proust's idiosyncrasies and cast aspersions about his nocturnal activities, betraying, to Proust's mind, the confidence of the close relation the men had formed in recent years. Proust was forgiving but undoubtedly hurt by Morand's thoughtlessness, suggesting to him that despite his claims to friendship, Morand had 'thrown [Proust] into the Hell that Dante reserved for his enemies' (*Corr.*, XVIII, 424).

The poem was published at a time when Proust's energies had once more been diverted from his work on the novel on to matters more mundane: the situation at rue Laurent-Pichat had worn him out and Réjane wanted to take back the apartment, so he moved house again on 1 October, settling this time for a fifth-floor apartment just a short distance away at 44 rue Hamelin. Soon enough, as Céleste puts it, life and the machinery of his habits resumed. The rings of the bell, the coffee in the afternoons, the late-night discussions, the work on the books, the silence. The only difference was that M. Proust went out less and less as he plunged ever deeper into his work and more and more he repeated 'I haven't much time, Céleste . . .'.[4]

But Proust received news at rue Hamelin on the afternoon of 10 December that placed great demands on his limited time. The Prix Goncourt had been awarded to *A l'ombre des jeunes filles*, the Academy choosing Proust's novel over Roland Dorgelès' *The Wooden Crosses* (a war novel by an ex-combattant) by six votes to four. Proust very seldom received unannounced visitors but on that afternoon he was woken by the arrival of Léon Daudet, a member of the Goncourt Academy, as well as Gallimard, Rivière and Gustave Tronche from the NRF, all of whom wished to share in celebrating this moment of recognition. Many laudatory press articles followed and Proust claimed to have received more than 800 letters of congratulation in the space of three days. He was delighted his work's quality had been recognized. There was, however, a significant current of feeling that the prize had gone to the wrong sort of work and the wrong sort of author. At 48, Proust was deemed to be too advanced in years (Dorgelès was 33): on 11 December *L'Humanité*'s headline read 'Make Way for the Old!' and with each article that appeared Proust's supposed age increased. Unable, because of his health and his regime (neither of which helped his case), to make the normal round of interviews in which he might correct such perceptions, and – he felt – ill supported in this by his publisher, the award of the prize was bittersweet. Although the publicity raised awareness and sales of *A l'ombre*, Dorgelès' book was by far the greater contemporary commercial success. Proust told a friend in mid-December that if he was able to find glasses to ease his painful eyes, then he would read Dorgelès' novel. After many years of complaining about his eyesight, Proust sent Céleste to an optician.[5]

She brought back a selection of spectacles with different lenses, and the sedentary novelist made his choice; it is not known whether Proust ever did read Dorgelès' book.

By the end of 1919 Proust had found fame but the sleep of the righteous still evaded him. He was relying on increasing quantities of uppers and downers (including Pantopon, a refined form of opium) to regulate his waking and (ever scarcer) sleeping hours (*Corr.*, xviii, 534). With the new year Proust was in print once more with another nrf publication: not an extract from the *Recherche* but an article, 'On Flaubert's style', celebrating the author's accomplishments, recently downplayed and indeed questioned by the critic Albert Thibaudet. Here is Proust at his critical best: when we read his discriminating appreciation of Flaubert's mastery of adverbs and prepositions we glimpse the delicate back-room manipulation of lexical weights and grammatical measures that underpins the final form of every Proustian sentence.[6]

The particular sentences being polished up at this stage were those of the first part of *The Guermantes Way*. Whilst in the process of correcting these proofs, in January 1920, Proust finally came to the realization that the proportions of what was still to be published ruled out his wish to see the remaining volumes appear all at once. He was worried about the availability of *Within a Budding Grove*, the securing of an English-language translator and his health (of course), and he was preoccupied with responding to criticisms of his work being published in the press. An article that appeared in English in *The Athenaeum* in April 1920 by Charles du Bos, one of Proust's most perceptive early commentators, sums up concisely the swirl of attention his work had drawn:

> The unexpectedness, the rich and manifold originality of M. Proust's work, took the public and the press unawares. They simply did not know what to do with it, so that there was nothing

left to them but to retaliate against the work and the man who reduced them to such an uncomfortable and undignified position. (*Corr.*, xix, 200–201, n. 4)

Some readers revelled in the shock of the new, however, and support came from what are now recognized as some of the most significant literary voices of the early twentieth century, among them Colette (who sent Proust *Chéri* in proof and expressed the wish that 'they would bring out a new Proust for my holidays'; *Corr.*, xix, 282) and the poet Natalie Clifford Barney, whom Proust never managed to meet but with whom he corresponded and exchanged publications. Despite the huge number of painstaking letters written, and many dictated to Rochat, responding to praise and countering various criticisms (of dilettantism, of being old-fashioned, of lacking structure, and so on), by mid-March Proust was able to return his corrected proofs of *The Guermantes Way i* to Gallimard. Wishing to speed the production process, the publisher hired help in the shape of a young poet by the name of André Breton. The following month, while he was working on Proust's text, Breton published *Les Champs magnétiques* (*The Magnetic Fields*), the first volume of Surrealist automatic writing, co-authored with Philippe Soupault. Breton went on to publish the *Manifesto of Surrealism* in 1924 and became a highly influential figure in the intellectual landscape of the twentieth century. A member of their group, Louis Aragon, had criticized Proust in *Littérature* in October 1919 but Breton himself – as Rivière put it to Proust – had declared 'an intense admiration for you, founded precisely on the poetic treasures that he has found in your work' (*Corr.*, xix, 337). Unfortunately, Breton was employed not to find poetic treasures but typos and in this he fell well short of the mark. When Proust received an advance copy of *The Guermantes Way i* in early September he was horrified to find more than 200 printing errors in just the first three-quarters of the volume. His handwritten errata ran to 23 pages.

At the time that Breton was working ineffectually on *The Guermantes Way*, Proust finally met with Sydney and Violet Schiff, a wealthy British couple, enthusiastic supporters of the arts (acquaintances of Eliot, Joyce, Wyndham Lewis, Katherine Mansfield and others) and passionate readers of Proust's work. They had corresponded since April 1919; the Schiffs had proposed that Proust spend time with them in London, to which he replied that he was 'unfortunately uninvitable' due the state of his health (*Corr.*, xviii, 196). It was Schiff who orchestrated the dinner at the Majestic Hotel in May 1922 at which, in the company of Picasso, Stravinsky and Diaghilev, Proust met James Joyce, although the ill health of one and the inebriation of the other meant that in reality the dinner was more a meeting *manqué* than a true meeting of minds.[7]

Proust was slowed somewhat by a painful bout of otitis caused by a Quiès ball (a medicated earplug) that became stuck in his ear at the start of September. This was one more discomfort to add to his growing list of ailments. He sensed more strongly than ever that his end was approaching. Despite the affront of the writer-diplomat's 'Ode', Proust had agreed to provide a preface for *Tendres stocks* (*Tender Stocks*), a collection of stories by Paul Morand. In the preface, which he drafted in September and October 1920, Proust's intimations of mortality are voiced wistfully and with characteristic elegance:

> A stranger has taken up residence in my brain. She came and she went; soon, from the whole way that she carried on, I knew her habits. What is more, as an over-solicitous lodger, she was anxious to enter into direct relations with me. I was surprised to find that she was not beautiful. I had always believed that Death was so. How otherwise would she get the better of us?[8]

He could not afford to dally, however, with his new lodger, nor gripe for long about the errors in the first volume of *The Guermantes*

*Way*: he had to move on to the proofs of *Guermantes II* and then
the opening of *Sodom and Gomorrah*, which he wished to publish
together in one volume, emphasizing the coherence of the *Recherche*
across its component parts. An announcement on 27 September,
however, shifted his focus somewhat (and brought yet more letters
to answer): Proust was named Chevalier de la Légion d'Honneur.
Earlier in the year both Henri de Régnier and Jacques Rivière had
tactfully warned Proust against putting himself forward for one of
the vacant chairs at the Académie Française ('they are not capable
of understanding you', wrote Rivière of the notoriously conservative
immortals, 'their sleep is too deep'; *Corr.*, XIX, 284). The Legion of
Honour may not have come with a ceremonial sword and cocked
hat but it was an accolade that pleased Proust; he asked if his
brother, by now Professor Proust and promoted to the rank of
Officier de la Légion d'Honneur, might be permitted to present
him his ribbon, the symbol of entry to a club to which their father,
the first Professor Proust, had belonged. With a little administrative string-pulling by Robert, permission was secured and on 7
November, without fanfare or fuss, Robert performed the duty at
Marcel's bedside before sharing dinner *à deux*, reminiscing about
their childhood.[9]

Just over a fortnight earlier *Le Côté de Guermantes I* had appeared,
too late for Colette's summer holiday but a most welcome arrival for
the growing numbers of Proustophiles awaiting the next instalment
of *A la recherche du temps perdu*. The greatest concentration of the
novel's society scenes, dealing with the beau monde and the lure
of the aristocracy, are found in this volume. For this reason, critics
found this a snobbish book and readers often skip it, but both
parties thereby miss the satire, the cutting and often highly amusing
critique of the vanity, hollowness and superficiality of society life
that is found in its pages. As well as being charged with snobbery,
*The Guermantes Way* was attacked for its style. Paul Souday, for
example, made his feelings plain in *Le Temps*: 'Marcel Proust is

above all a nervous aesthete, somewhat morbid, almost *feminine*'
(*Corr.*, XIX, 576, n. 12). 'There is only a short step from "feminine"
to "effeminate"', countered Proust, all too aware how this veiled
insinuation would be interpreted; but with volumes already
announced under the title *Sodom and Gomorrah*, he recognized
that his scope for self-defence was limited. He would have to let
his work, in its own time, speak for itself. Indeed, we can perceive
Proust's longer-term hopes for his novel between the lines of his
response, in December, to a survey about 'Romanticism and
Classicism' carried out for a literary journal:

> We cannot doubt that innovators worthy of becoming classics
> obey a severe inner discipline and are above all else constructors,
> but precisely because their architecture is new, it can happen
> that it goes for a long time unrecognized.[10]

By the end of 1920 Proust was increasingly unwell. Severe asthma
attacks in October 1920 had led Dr Bize to administer morphine
injections ('which did nothing but make me completely numb';
*Corr.*, XIX, 518). Self-medication, performed in search of sleep in
late November, hit the extremes of 'a whole box of cachets of
Veronal in one go, at the same time as Dial and opium', although
without reward: 'I haven't slept but I've suffered terribly' (*Corr.*,
XIX, 618). Proust insisted in the same letter to Natalie Barney that
he 'love[d] dearly the awful life on to which I hang by no more
than a thread', yet he seemed quite impervious to the fact that such
pharmaceutical roulette was wearing that thread down to the finest
of filaments, which would eventually, ineluctably, snap.

Yet somehow the thread held: concealed heroics of kidneys,
liver, blood and brain meant that Proust's sunken eyes kept pace
over his increasingly spidery lines of text, his stiffened hands kept
pen and paper in concert and on 1 January 1921, another New
Year's edition of the NRF carried an excerpt from his novel, this time

one of the most arrestingly moving passages of the *Recherche*, the death of the grandmother from *Guermantes II*. And the material kept coming: the February *NRF* carried another excerpt; Morand's *Tendres stocks*, prefaced by Proust, appeared later that month; then in March, the result of what Proust himself acknowledged to have been a 'colossal' labour, he submitted to Gallimard the corrected proofs for *The Guermantes Way II* and *Sodom and Gomorrah I*. When this instalment appeared, half of the *Recherche* would be in print and the possibility of the project's completion would be just that little bit closer.

Not content, however, to concentrate solely on *A la recherche*, Proust worked in April and May on an essay for the *NRF* on Baudelaire, a homage to mark the poet's centenary. Baudelaire, along with Vigny, was 'the greatest poet of the nineteenth century' for Proust; his verses are quoted and alluded to throughout the *Recherche* and the poet's themes – the body, memory, love, desire, the temptation of evil, death – are those of Proust's novel. Reading 'Concerning Baudelaire', which appeared in the June 1921 edition of the *NRF*, reminds us of the strong affinity between the two writers. Baudelaire's fascination with lesbianism, for example, can be seen to underpin the Albertine narrative and subtly to underwrite the very notion of the '*jeunes filles en fleurs*'. '*Car Lesbos entre tous m'a choisi sur la terre*', wrote Baudelaire, quoted by Proust in his essay, '*Pour chanter le secret de ses vierges en fleurs*' (For Lesbos has chosen me amongst all on earth / To sing the secret of its flowering virgins).[11]

Baudelaire is one of Proust's most important literary touchstones. In visual art too there are artists that hold a special place in his personal pantheon, Rembrandt and Chardin among them. But the creator of what was in Proust's view the most beautiful picture in the world was a then little known Dutch painter: Johannes Vermeer (1632–1675). In late spring of 1921 the picture in question, the *View of Delft*, came to Paris as part of a visiting exhibition, nineteen years after Proust had first seen it in The Hague. Having read an

Proust in 1921,
probably on his
visit to the Musée
de Jeu de Paume
exhibition.

article about the exhibition that made particular mention of Vermeer's painting and encouraged by Morand, who claimed to have persuaded the exhibition organizers to include the *View of Delft* because he knew how much it meant to Proust, sometime between 18 and 24 May the author, in rather a fragile state, made the trip to the Musée du Jeu de Paume to see it again for himself. In *The Captive* a similar set of events unfolds for Bergotte, with the difference that the fictional writer breathes his last in front of Vermeer's canvas after recognizing only too late the lessons that the finest details of the picture offered his own approach to art. Proust's correspondence around this time suggests that he was not in quite such an extreme state of ill health as Bergotte at the exhibition, but a comment in a letter about worries of having an attack and his sudden death 'becoming the sensational news story of the exhibition' (*Corr.*, xx, 251) show how his fiction might be seen as the articulation of his worst fears. The pages on the writer's death, in which this concern is directly voiced by Bergotte, and the pages that follow, which discuss the possibility that his novels, living on after his bodily demise, might represent 'the symbol of his resurrection' (*The Captive*,

Johannes Vermeer, *View of Delft, c.* 1660, oil on canvas.

209; iii, 693), are often cited to illustrate Proust's hopes for the work to whose creation his existence was devoted. The pages preceding Bergotte's death are less well known, yet they merit citing for the intriguing perspective they provide on Proust's relation to medicine:

> Maddened by uninterrupted pain, to which was added insomnia broken only by brief spells of nightmare, Bergotte called in no more doctors and tried with success, but to excess, different narcotics, trustingly reading the prospectus that accompanied each of them, a prospectus which proclaimed the necessity of sleep but hinted that all the preparations which induce it (except the one around which the prospectus was wrapped, which never produced any toxic effect) were toxic, and therefore made the remedy worse than the disease. Bergotte tried them all. (*The Captive*, 206; iii, 691)

In the month preceding the exhibition at the Jeu de Paume, Proust was taking morphine, aspirin, adrenalin and other substances, although the result, he told Hauser 'so far is weak' (*Corr.*, xx, 163).

Any new publication brought with it a liberal dose of anxiety for Proust. The publication on 2 May of the volume formed of *The Guermantes Way ii* and *Sodom and Gomorrah i* was particularly fraught for the author: in reaching the novel's halfway point readers now arrived at the cities of the plain and Proust's fullest exposition and exploration of human sexuality. Léon Daudet explained to Proust that his paper *L'Action française* was not even willing to print the title *Sodom and Gomorrah* for fear of offending its readers. François Mauriac, upon reading the first part of *Sodom*, felt 'all the most contradictory sentiments: admiration, repulsion, terror, disgust . . .' (*Corr.*, xx, 209) and chided Proust for his candour: 'I shudder, my friend . . . thinking of all those who closed their eyes so as not to see themselves and whose secret and shameful wound you are probing with a brutal finger' (*Corr.*, xx, 269). Proust wished to offer an objective portrayal of sexuality – he sought to present what could be observed in the world without passing judgement on it. *Sodom and Gomorrah* opens with a sexual encounter between two men, but there are many individuals in *A la recherche* (Odette, Albertine, Saint-Loup and Morel, for example, to name only the most prominent) who have sexual relations with both men and women. A problem with Proust's view of the individual's sexuality as a fluid entity capable of alteration during a given lifetime is that it ran counter to dominant scientific and moral discourses of the time, which largely considered same-sex relations as illness, aberration or vice.[12]

It was not only the straight, or the strait-laced, who objected to *Sodom and Gomorrah*, however. André Gide's view of male homosexuality diverged significantly from Proust's and what he found in *Sodom and Gomorrah* he considered to be stigmatizing and condemnatory. 'A pederast (in the most Greek sense of the word)', wrote Gide, 'will never agree to recognize himself in the depiction you offer of inverts' (*Corr.*, xx, 241). Gide had written four dialogues as an apologia for the naturalness of what he termed 'pederasty' – relations between men that have nothing to do with 'inversion, effeminacy or sodomy' – entitled *Corydon*, which had been anonymously printed in a short run and privately circulated between 1911 and 1920.[13] As William Carter summarizes, 'for Gide, a man in love with another man carried on a noble tradition that dated back to the ancient Greeks, whereas a man like Charlus, who wanted to be a woman for another man, represented a decadent variety of homosexuals'.[14] Gide lent Proust a copy of *Corydon* but it made no difference. 'It isn't my fault', wrote Proust, 'if M. de Charlus is an old gentleman; I can't suddenly give him the appearance of a Sicilian shepherd' (*Corr.*, xx, 272). Gide and Proust had a number of late-night conversations in May that treated the topic of sexuality. In his journal Gide claims that Proust reproached himself for 'the "indecision" that caused him, in order to sustain the heterosexual part of his book, to transpose to the *jeunes filles en fleurs* all that had been graceful, tender and charming in his homosexual memories, such that for him all that remains of Sodom are traits that are grotesque and abject'. In his journal entry for the same day, Gide notes Proust's comment that he 'had only ever liked women spiritually and had only ever known love with men'.[15] However significant we take this reported comment to be, it is clear from reading Proust's novel that sexuality in the *Recherche* is about a lot more than just desire between men. Proust explores the nature of love, the role physical desire plays in it, the ways in which we are tortured by possessiveness and our attempts (normally quite fruit-less) to 'know' or 'understand' the objects of our desire, regardless of their sex. *Sodom and Gomorrah* may take sexual inversion as its central focus, but it is important not to lose sight of the fact that *A la recherche* as a whole is interested in *human* relations in all their great diversity and those traits that we all share – desire, jealousy, insecurity, passion – regardless of our sexual orientation.

Proust's bodily ills continued. His difficulties speaking, which his brother put down to poisoning from the combination of drugs Proust was consuming, troubled him in the spring of 1921. The remedy Marcel administered to himself? 'Caffeine and adrenalin' (*Corr.*, xx, 195). The summer that year was so stiflingly hot in Paris that the 14 July parades were cancelled, yet in August Proust was writing to Jacques Boulenger 'from [his] bed, under seven woollen covers, with a fur, three hot water bottles, and a fire burning' (*Corr.*, xx, 413). Proust, who caused heads to turn in earlier years by keep-ing his coat on in the dining room at the Ritz, appeared to be more sensitive than ever to the cold (doubtless due to poor circulation), a state evoked in the lines describing Bergotte's last days:

> He would apologize . . . to the few friends whom he allowed to
> penetrate to his sanctuary; pointing to his tartan plaids, his

travelling-rugs, he would say merrily: 'After all, my dear fellow, life, as Anaxagoras has said, is a journey.' Thus he went on growing steadily colder, a tiny planet offering a prophetic image of the greater, when gradually heat will withdraw from the earth, then life itself. (*The Captive*, 204; III, 689)

Proust came close to his moment of extinction in October when he mixed up his dosages and took seven, rather than 0.7 grams of Veronal. Again, incredibly, he pulled through, even joking to Gallimard in a letter the following day that he was glad to have survived so as not to keep his editor waiting for his corrections to *Sodom and Gomorrah II*.

While Proust was struggling to stay upright in rue Hamelin with bouts of dizziness in September and October 1921, in London a young Scot named C. K. Scott Moncrieff made an important decision. He had been seriously injured leading his battalion in a major offensive in 1917. While working in London in the War Office and then as private secretary to the owner of *The Times*, Lord North-cliffe, Scott Moncrieff had started translating. His *Chanson de Roland* (1919) and *Beowulf* (1921) had been received very positively. Having recently discovered Proust, he now decided to leave his post with Lord Northcliffe in order to devote himself full time to the task of translating *A la recherche* into English. His decision, however, did not meet with universal approval. Sir Edmund Gosse, one of England's most important critics of the late nineteenth and early twentieth centuries, wrote to Scott Moncrieff. 'Since you told me you were translating Proust I have not felt happy', he wrote:

I cannot be charged with prejudice, since (unless I make a great mistake) I was the first in England, and one of the first anywhere, to recognize the exciting quality in *Chez Swann*. But I do not feel sure that that quality is really first rate, is going to be durable. It has flattered us by pandering to some very ephemeral things, to the amusement of having our literature in powder, instead of in blocks and slabs . . . [Proust] is a monstrously clever fellow, but I grudge months of your best life spent in shaking these French powders into your English box. You were born for much better things.[16]

Gosse's casting of Proust as slight and ephemeral is so diametrically opposed to our contemporary view of Proust as the *ne plus ultra* of literary heavyweights as to be amusing. And his avuncular warnings came a little late – Scott Moncrieff already had a contract that had been agreed between Chatto & Windus and Gallimard, with Proust's approval, a detail that repeatedly slipped Proust's mind in his final years. When Scott Moncrieff's first volume appeared in October 1922, neither Schiff (jealous, for he believed himself to be the only suitable translator of the author he so idolized) nor Proust realized that the overall title 'Remembrance of Things Past' was a borrowing from Shakespeare's Sonnet 30, and Schiff misinformed Proust how 'Swann's Way' might translate back into French. As a result, Proust railed to Gallimard about how he would not stand for his work being 'demolished by Englishmen' (*Corr.*, XXI, 476) and – in French – wrote a somewhat curt letter (the only one he ever wrote) to Scott Moncrieff. The translator replied briefly, in English: 'my knowledge of French is too imperfect, too stunted a growth', he wrote, 'for me to weave from it the chapelet that I would fain offer you' (*Corr.*, XXI, 501). So while Scott Moncrieff's labours, from 1921 until his death in 1930, have served anglophone readers for well over 80 years, they were undertaken without any assistance from the author.

In 1920 Jacques Blanche had heard of a London 'Marcel Proust Club' being founded in Chelsea. The following year in July another acquaintance told Proust that in London 'the "intellectual" ladies have two subjects of conversation. The scientifically minded talk about Einstein, of course. The literary types talk of "Prr . . . oust"'

(*Corr.*, xx, 388). And it was not solely around London's coffee tables that Proust and Einstein were being spoken of in the same breath. In June and in August 1922, the NRF published articles by Roger Allard and Camille Vettard suggesting that, with their theories of relativity and handling of narrative time and the experience of memory, physicist and novelist alike had reshaped their respective fields – and the way we look at the world – in a similarly radical fashion.[17] And this renown was spreading. Valéry Larbaud, translator of Coleridge, Whitman and Joyce and a key figure in the development of European modernism, described Proust's as 'the most important work in the French language' of their times (*Corr.*, xx, 392). In late 1921 the academic, historian and critic Bernard Faÿ met with Proust, explaining that he had students at New York's Columbia University, where he taught for part of the year, who wished to write dissertations on Proust's work. In February 1922 the influential German critic Ernst Robert Curtius published his first essay on the *Recherche* in *Der Neue Merkur* and started to correspond with Proust; in June, Spain's foremost critic José Ortega y Gasset lectured on Proust in Madrid; and T. S. Eliot sought material from Proust for his new journal *The Criterion*; the first number appeared in October 1922 without work by Proust but carrying a new poem by Eliot: 'The Waste Land'.

Proust ended 1921 with rheumatic pain and fever. Each letter in the new year explained the effort (and medication) required just to put pen to paper. To ease the situation, in February (the month that Joyce's *Ulysses* was published in Paris) Proust took on Yvonne Albaret, Céleste's niece, to type up the *cahiers* containing what at the time was *Sodome et Gomorrhe III* – the volumes we now know as *The Captive* and *The Fugitive*. Editing *The Captive* proved extremely arduous – so voluminous were his changes and additions that it was retyped three times over. While this work was ongoing, the printers were hard at work finalizing *Sodom and Gomorrah II*, which appeared on 29 April in three volumes (in part due to slightly larger type to make reading easier). Publicity notices for the book bore the quaint rider 'Not to be read by young girls'. Where Gide had been cool (at best) about the first part of *Sodom and Gomorrah*, Mme Straus and Cocteau were effusive about the second. 'Next to your books everything seems boring', wrote Cocteau (*Corr.*, XXI, 214). Rivière, for his part, marvelled at Proust's 'extraordinary faculty of analysis': the way he shows the narrator's love for Albertine growing out of his jealousy was, for Rivière, 'quite the most prodigious thing' (*Corr.*, XX, 488).

Two days after the publication of *Sodom and Gomorrah II*, Proust suffered from yet another pharmaceutical blunder. He damaged his alimentary canal by taking undiluted adrenalin, leaving himself in excruciating pain and able to consume only ice cream that Céleste's husband Odilon fetched from the Ritz. He did manage, on 18 May, to make it to the Schiffs' dinner celebrating the premiere of Stravinsky's *Renard*, the fateful (or, rather, uneventful) 'Night at the Majestic' in the company of Picasso, Joyce and others. And despite his discomfort, work continued: around this time Proust decided that, rather than *Sodom and Gomorrah II* and *III*, the next volumes should have differentiated titles of their own, and he initially proposed *La Prisonnière* and *La Fugitive*. A little later the publication of a collection of verse by the Bengali Nobel Prize winner Rabindranath Tagore, translated as *La Fugitive*, put Proust off this latter title and thus he opted, in the end, for *Albertine disparue*.

Revising proof copy or typescripts was for Proust always a process of accretion, of sedimentation, of splicing and overlay. Pasted-on strips of paper added new dimensions to his pages once all the margins were darkened with ink: here are the eddies and overflows of what Walter Benjamin in his brilliant short essay on Proust referred to as 'the Nile of language'.[18] Alluding to the typescript prepared by Yvonne Albaret of the Albertine volumes, Proust described the work he still had to do in 1922 as '*le travail de réfection . . . où j'ajoute partout et change tout*' (the work of reshaping

The bulging mass of the final manuscript notebook, 'Cahier xx'.

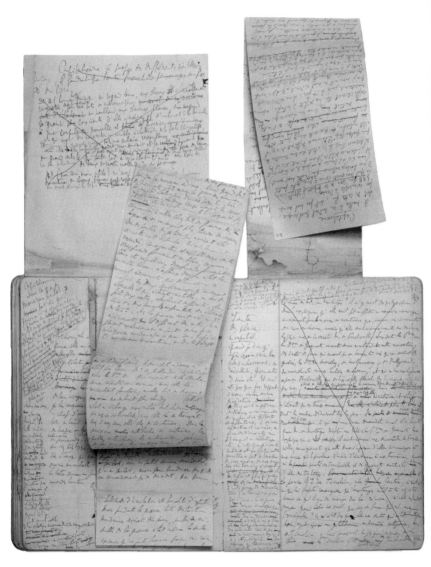

The organic proliferation of text: manuscript pages and paste-ons of *Time Regained*.

. . . where I make additions everywhere and change everything; *Corr.*, xxi, 310). All this made it a huge surprise, therefore, when a typescript of *Albertine disparue* was discovered in 1986 bearing notes in Proust's hand indicating major cuts that would reduce that volume by approximately two-thirds of its original length. What is more, the place of Albertine's death is moved from the Touraine to the banks of the Vivonne near Montjouvain (and thus in proximity to Mlle Vinteuil and her lesbian companion) – a far clearer indication of Albertine's reasons for flight than is offered by the published version of the text.[19] Proust had indicated to Gallimard that *Sodom and Gomorrah* might extend to as many as six parts (*Corr.*, xxi, 39); it is highly likely, therefore, that the material marked for excision from this version of the text would, as was Proust's habit, have been grafted elsewhere in those hypothetical future volumes following *The Fugitive* and preceding *Time Regained*. But time got the better of Proust: on 30 October or 1 November he sent Gallimard the corrected typescript of *The Captive* from which proofs were to be prepared, but before he could correct those or complete revisions to the remainder of the novel, the tenuous thread by which he had held on to life at last gave way; after his death the copy of the typescript from which the first posthumous editions of *The Fugitive* were prepared was not that bearing the author's radical changes.

In early September Proust reported suffering a number of falls in his room. His breathing was troubled, eating was difficult and sleep was rare. Forssgren returned from the United States and tracked down Proust, requesting a rendezvous. Proust made the effort to go to Forssgren's hotel but, despite a long wait, the Swede did not appear. Forssgren believed that it was the chill Proust caught during his wait in the draughty lobby that caused his final illness and death, but this is quite unlikely. In 1919 Proust had described how his asthma attacks left him 'gasping like someone half-drowned who is pulled out of the water, without being able to

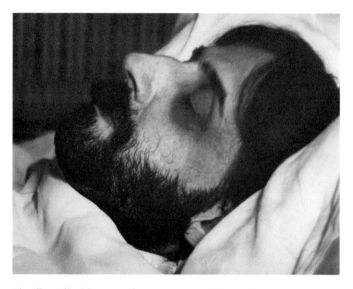

The effects of his labours are plain to see on Proust's face in this deathbed photograph taken by Man Ray, 1922.

utter a word or make a movement' (*Corr.*, XVIII, 466), and such was his condition towards the end of October when a dose of flu aggravated his asthma. Dr Bize and Robert Proust tried to convince Marcel to take treatment, to spend some time in a clinic or simply to accept injections of camphorated oil intended to ease his congested lungs, but Proust refused. Despite being the son and brother of revered doctors, to the very end he persisted in following only his own medical advice. Weak but angered by their meddling, after Bize and his brother were gone Proust told Céleste not to let them return.[20] Flu gave way to bronchitis and the pneumonia Bize had feared soon manifested itself.

Around midnight between 17 and 18 November, Proust rang for Céleste and expressed his wish that they continue to work.[21] He started dictating, and they carried on this way for two hours; when the effort to speak was too much, Proust continued his corrections

Proust on his deathbed, sketch by Dunoyer de Segonzac, 1922.

and additions by hand until half-past-three in the morning. Some hours later, Proust suffered hallucinations of a 'horrible big fat woman dressed in black' who was in his room, a delirious manifestation, perhaps, of the 'lodger' who had taken up residence in his mind some months before. After this, Céleste decided to call Bize. It was around 10 a.m. when he arrived and gave Proust an injection to ease his pain. Later Robert arrived, followed by Professor Babinski. Proust was given oxygen but the three doctors could see that there was no more that they could do. Bize and Babinski departed, leaving Robert and Céleste by Proust's bedside.

He had not left Paris since 1914 and he had scarcely left his bed for weeks, yet here, for all his neuroses and idiosyncrasies and despite the limitations imposed on him by his health, Proust had, as Rivière put it, 'given body to the multitudinousness of life itself' (*Corr.*, XXI, 376). Simultaneously, Proust had provided what one of his best modern critics has called 'a portrait of a single, intensely perceptive and reflective mind'.[22] Proust's creation, this astonishing work, at once expansive and inward-turned, had required a devotion that was all-consuming. Towards the close of *Time Regained* Proust's narrator speaks of how an artist's commitment to his work might be thought of as 'an egotism which could be put to work for the benefit of other people' (*Time Regained*, 436; IV, 613). Proust's work had taken his health, ruined his eyesight. Robert leaned forward and gently closed his brother's eyes. Marcel would see no more, but the work he had created by dint of his single-mindedness would be 'a kind of optical instrument' for generations of curious minds, enabling each reader 'to discern what, without this book, he would perhaps never have perceived in himself' (*Time Regained*, 273; IV, 489–90).

# References

## Introduction

1 *Le Carnet de 1908*, ed. Philip Kolb, *Cahiers Marcel Proust*, n. s., 8 (Paris, 1976), p. 64.
2 Ibid., p. 83.

## 1 Physician Heal thy Son

1 Daniel Panzac, *Le Docteur Adrien Proust: Père méconnu, précurseur oublié* (Paris, 2003), p. 44.
2 Evelyne Bloch-Dano, *Mme Proust : Biographie* (Paris, 2004), p. 79.
3 'Days of Reading (I)', in *Against Sainte-Beuve and Other Essays*, trans. John Sturrock (Harmondsworth, 1988), pp. 195–226 (195); *Contre Sainte-Beuve précédé de pastiches et mélanges et suivi de essais et articles*, ed. Pierre Clarac and Yves Sandre (Paris, 1971), pp. 160–94 (160).
4 Robert Proust, 'Marcel Proust intime', in *Hommage à Marcel Proust, 1871–1922*, *Nouvelle Revue Française* (January 1923), pp. 24–26 (24).
5 'Retour à Guermantes' ('Return to Guermantes'), in *Contre Sainte-Beuve suivi de nouveaux mélanges* (Paris, 1954), pp. 284–300 (295). The subsequent quotations from this text are from pp. 295–6.
6 *Hommage à Marcel Proust*, p. 24
7 *L'Indifférent*, ed. Philip Kolb (Paris, 1978), p. 43.
8 William C. Carter, *Marcel Proust*: *A Life* (New Haven, CT, and London, 2000), p. 815, n. 71.
9 Bernard Straus, *The Maladies of Marcel Proust: Doctors and Disease in his Life and Work* (New York, 1980), p. 163.

10 André Maurois, *The Quest for Proust*, trans. Gerard Hopkins (London, 1950), p. 22.

## 2 Asthmatic Absentee / Marcel *Militaire*

1 The standard work on this period of Proust's life is André Ferré, *Les Années de collège de Marcel Proust* (Paris, 1959). For a rich and informative survey of the structures, benefits and drawbacks of secondary education in the Third French Republic, see Theodore Zeldin, 'Logic and Verbalism', in *A History of French Passions: France, 1848–1945*, vol. III: *Intellect and Pride* (Oxford, 1977), pp. 205–42.
2 *Hommage à Marcel Proust, 1871–1922, Nouvelle Revue Française* (January 1923), p. 28.
3 Richard Ellmann, 'Literary Biography', in *Golden Codgers: Biographical Speculations* (New York and London, 1973), pp. 1–16 (4).
4 Ferré, *Les Années de collège*, p. 65.
5 Ibid., p. 250.
6 The full questionnaire is reproduced in William Carter, *Marcel Proust: A Life* (New Haven, CT, and London, 2000), pp. 52–3.
7 W. B. Yeats, 'Essays and Introductions', quoted in Hermione Lee, *Biography: A Very Short Introduction* (Oxford, 2009), p. 93
8 Jean-Yves Tadié, *Marcel Proust: Biographie* (Paris, 1996), p. 69.
9 *Hommage à Marcel Proust*, p. 42.
10 Carter, *Marcel Proust*, p. 68.
11 Malcolm Bowie, *Proust Among the Stars* (London, 1998), p. 230.
12 Marcel Proust, *Écrits de jeunesse, 1887–1895*, ed. Anne Borrel (Illiers-Combray, 1991), pp. 164–5.
13 Ibid., p. 167.

## 3 Undergraduate, Critic, Duellist

1 Proust's unfinished novel, entitled *Jean Santeuil* by its posthumous editors, was translated by Gerard Hopkins (New York and London, 1955); the French text used by Hopkins has since been superseded by the 'Pléiade' edition edited by Pierre Clarac and Yves Sandre (Paris,

1971). The passage quoted is from p. 190 of the French edition; it does not feature in Hopkins's translation.

2  Jacques-Emile Blanche, *Mes modèles: Barrès, Hardy, Proust, James, Gide, Moore* (Paris, 1928), p. 108.

3  See Jeanne Pouquet, *Le Salon de Mme Arman de Caillavet* (Paris, 1926), pp. 107–8.

4  Fernand Gregh, *L'Age d'or: Souvenirs d'enfance et de jeunesse* (Paris, 1947), p. 326.

5  Robert de Billy, *Marcel Proust: Lettres et conversations* (Paris, 1930), p. 22.

6  *Le Banquet* (Geneva, Slatkine Reprints, 1971), p. 5.

7  For the full text of the second questionnaire, see *Against Sainte-Beuve and Other Essays*, trans. John Sturrock (Harmondsworth, 1988), pp. 113–14; *Contre Sainte-Beuve précédé de pastiches et mélanges et suivi de essais et articles*, ed. Pierre Clarac and Yves Sandre (Paris, 1971), 336–7.

8  On Proust's debt to the writings of Ribot and the relation of the writings of Proust *père et fils*, see Michael R. Finn, *Proust, the Body and Literary Form* (Cambridge, 1999), in particular chapter One, 'Proust between neurasthenia and hysteria'.

9  Publication figure from Alain Pagès and Owen Morgan, *Guide Emile Zola* (Paris, 2002), p. 301; *Le Figaro* quoted in Robert Gildea, *Children of the Revolution: The French, 1799–1914* (London, 2008), p. 403.

10  J. Picon, 'La Revue blanche', in *Dictionnaire Marcel Proust*, ed. Annick Bouillaguet and Brian G. Rogers (Paris, 2004), p. 872.

11  Quoted in Bernard Gavoty, *Reynaldo Hahn: Musicien de la Belle Epoque* (Paris, 1976), p. 89.

12  *Hommage à Marcel Proust, 1871–1922*, *Nouvelle Revue Française* (January 1923), pp. 39–40.

13  Lucien Daudet, *Autour de soixante lettres de Marcel Proust*, *Cahiers Marcel Proust*, 5 (Paris, 1929), pp. 30–31.

14  Léon Blum, quoted in *Les Plaisirs et les jours*, ed. Thierry Laget (Paris, 1993), p. 293.

15  George Painter, *Marcel Proust: A Biography*, vol. i (London, 1959), p. 208.

16  Lorrain reproduced in Leighton Hodson, ed., *Marcel Proust: The Critical Heritage* (London, 1989), p. 67.

17  Painter, *Marcel Proust*, vol. i, p. 209.

18  William C. Carter, *Proust in Love* (New Haven, CT, and London, 2006), p. 58.

## 4 Intellectual, Translator, Mourner

1 For much of the detail of the Affair I draw here on Ruth Harris's excellent study *The Man on Devil's Island: Alfred Dreyfus and the Affair that Divided France* (London, 2010).

2 William C. Carter, *Marcel Proust: A Life* (New Haven, CT, and London, 2000), p. 252.

3 Jean-Yves Tadié, *Marcel Proust: Biographie* (Paris, 1996), p. 350.

4 See Céleste Albaret, *Monsieur Proust* (Paris, 1973), p. 220.

5 Marie Nordlinger, preface to *Lettres à une amie: Recueil de quarante-et-une lettres inédites adressées à Marie Nordlinger, 1899–1908* (Manchester, 1942), p. ix.

6 Ibid.

7 Léon Daudet, *Souvenirs littéraires* (Paris, 1968), p. 221.

8 Gertrude Stein, *Paris France* [1940] (London, 1983), p. 11.

9 See 'Ça prend', *Magazine littéraire* (January 1979), collected in Roland Barthes, *Œuvres complètes*, ed. Eric Marty (Paris, 1993–95), vol. III, pp. 993–4.

10 Carter, *Marcel Proust*, p. 283.

11 For a fuller treatment of this trip, see my article '"Un peu fatigué (et cependant très bien portant)": Santé et souffrance du voyage en Hollande à la *Recherche du temps perdu*', in *Proust et la Hollande: Marcel Proust Aujourd'hui*, 8 (2011), pp. 25–35.

12 Evelyne Bloch-Dano, *Madame Proust: A Biography*, trans. Alice Kaplan (Chicago and London, 2007), pp. 224–5.

13 Nordlinger, *Lettres à une amie*, p. x.

## 5 Beginnings and Endings

1 Philippe Sollers' beautifully illustrated *L'œil de Proust: Les Dessins de Marcel Proust* (Paris, 1999) gives many reproductions of Proust's inexpert but intriguing drawings.

2 See Theodore Zeldin, *A History of French Passions: France, 1848–1945*, vol. IV: *Taste and Corruption* (Oxford, 1973–7), p. 289.

3 *Le Carnet de 1908*, ed. Philip Kolb, *Cahiers Marcel Proust*, n. s., 8 (Paris, 1976), p. 53.

4 Ibid., pp. 60–61.

5 For a bold, persuasive reading of Proust's novel that rejects the 'boys in drag' argument, see Elisabeth Ladenson's excellent *Proust's Lesbianism* (Ithaca, NY, and London, 1999).

6 For a detailed summary see Jean-Yves Tadié, *Marcel Proust: Biographie* (Paris, 1996), p. 669. Readers interested in the material development of Proust's novel should consult Florence Callu's invaluable notes 'Le Fonds Proust de la Bibliothèque nationale' in the first volume of the Pléiade edition (I, cxlv–clxix) and the digitized versions of this material on the website of the Institut des Textes et Manuscrits Modernes (ITEM): see 'Fonds Proust numérique', www.item.ens.fr, accessed 29 March 2012.

## 6 *Swann* Published and Alfred *Disparu*

1 See Jean-Yves Tadié, *Marcel Proust: Biographie* (Paris, 1996), pp. 671–4.

2 Lucien Daudet, 'Transpositions', in *Hommage à Marcel Proust, 1871–1922*, *Nouvelle Revue Française* (January 1923), p. 50.

3 For a clear and concise study of the publishing history of *A la recherche*, see Christine Cano's highly readable *Proust's Deadline* (Urbana, IL, and Chicago, 2006).

4 'Swann's First Critic: A Confidential Report', in *Marcel Proust: The Critical Heritage*, ed. Leighton Hodson (London and New York, 1989), pp. 75–6.

5 Hodson, ed., *Marcel Proust*, p. 81.

6 See Louis de Robert, *Comment débuta Marcel Proust* (Paris, 1969), p. 9.

7 For wide-ranging surveys of the exceptional riches of this fateful year, see Jean-Michel Rabaté, *1913: The Cradle of Modernism* (Oxford, 2007) and Virginia Cowles, *1913: The Defiant Swan-song* (London, 1967).

8 Tadié, *Marcel Proust: Biographie*, p. 704.

9 Hodson, ed., *Marcel Proust*, p. 83.

## 7 The Great War

1 William C. Carter, *Marcel Proust: A Life* (New Haven, CT, and London, 2000), p. 581.

2 Jean-Yves Tadié, *Marcel Proust: Biographie* (Paris, 1996), p. 735.

3 William C. Carter, ed., *The Memoirs of Ernest A. Forssgren, Proust's Swedish Valet* (New Haven, CT, and London, 2006).

4 On Proust's wartime reading, see Christine Cano's essay 'Proust and the Wartime Press', in '*Le Temps retrouvé' Eighty Years After / 80 ans après: Critical Essays / Essais critiques*, ed. Adam Watt (Oxford and Bern, 2009), pp. 133–40.

5 For an insightful study of Proust's relation to questions of patriotism, see Edward Hughes's excellent *Proust, Class and Nation* (Oxford, 2011).

6 For a rewarding consideration of Proust's work in relation to the cathedral as a structural model, see Luc Fraisse's major study *L'œuvre cathédrale: Proust et l'architecture médiévale* (Paris, 1990).

7 We know this since his name features in a recently discovered police report of a raid on the establishment in January 1918: see Laure Murat, 'Proust, Marcel, 46 ans, rentier: Un individu "aux allures de pédéraste" fiché à la police', *Revue littéraire*, XIV (2005), pp. 82–93.

8 Céleste Albaret, *Monsieur Proust* (Paris, 1973), p. 240.

9 For a transcription of the notes from Jouhandeau's *carnet*, see Henri Bonnet, *Les Amours et la sexualité de Marcel Proust* (Paris, 1985), pp. 79–80.

10 Readers interested in the relationship between Proust and Gallimard should consult Pascal Fouché, ed., *Correspondance avec Gaston Gallimard* (Paris, 1989).

11 A growing number of works on Proust and music exists: see Françoise Leriche, 'Musique', in *Dictionnaire Marcel Proust*, ed. A. Bouillaguet and B. Rogers (Paris, 2004), pp. 664–6; and Julian Johnson, 'Music', in *Marcel Proust in Context*, ed. Adam Watt (Cambridge, forthcoming).

12 See 'Souvenirs de Gaston Poulet et Amable Massis', *Bulletin des Amis de Marcel Proust*, 11 (1961), pp. 424–8.

13 Albaret, *Monsieur Proust*, p. 398.

14 See Paul Morand, *Journal d'un attaché d'ambassade, 1916–1917* (Paris, 1996), pp. 150–51; and Albaret, *Monsieur Proust*, pp. 114–15.

15 It is not entirely clear what made up these 'four volumes': Kolb
suggests that they 'must have been' *Pastiches et mélanges*; the two
volumes of *The Guermantes Way*; and *Sodom and Gomorrah I* (note 4
to *Corr.*, XVII, 503). It seems more likely that the fourth volume was
the first printing of *Budding Grove*, completed on 30 November 1918.
Carter takes this line (*Marcel Proust: A Life*, p. 678); Tadié simply notes
Proust's comment that he received four volumes of proofs to correct
without specifying which (*Marcel Proust: Biographie*, p. 807), although
he misquotes the letter in question.

16 Albaret, *Monsieur Proust*, p. 184.

17 For a detailed account of Proust's time with Rochat between 1918
and 1921, see William C. Carter, *Proust in Love* (New Haven, CT, and
London, 2006), pp. 159–80.

18 Carter, *Proust in Love*, p. 168.

19 See Tadié, *Marcel Proust: Biographie*, pp. 782–3.


## 8 Recognition and Decline

1 Albaret dates this moment to the early spring of 1922 but, as we have
seen in relation to other events, her memory was not infallible. See
Céleste Albaret, *Monsieur Proust* (Paris, 1973), pp. 399–404.

2 Ibid., pp. 403–4.

3 On the burning of the *cahiers*, see ibid., pp. 324–6.

4 Ibid., p. 390.

5 Ibid., p. 322.

6 See 'On Flaubert's Style', in *Against Sainte-Beuve and Other Essays*,
trans. John Sturrock (Harmondsworth, 1988), pp. 262–74, hereafter
*ASB*; *Contre Sainte-Beuve précédé de pastiches et mélanges et suivi de
essais et articles*, ed. Pierre Clarac and Yves Sandre (Paris, 1971),
pp. 586–600, hereafter *CSB*.

7 For further details see Richard Davenport Hines, *A Night at the Majestic:
Proust and the Great Modernist Dinner Party of 1922* (London, 2006).

8 'Preface to Morand', in *ASB*, 275–85 (275); *CSB*, 606–16 (606).

9 Albaret, *Monsieur Proust*, p. 370.

10 'Classicism and Romanticism', in *CSB*, 617–18 (617); also in *Corr.*, XIX,
643.

11 See 'Concerning Baudelaire', in *ASB*, 286–309 (302); *CSB*, 618–39 (633).

12 For a recent assessment of homosexuality in Proust's novel and works by his contemporaries, see Michael Lucey, *Never Say 'I': Sexuality and the First Person in Colette, Gide and Proust* (Durham, NC, 2006).

13 André Gide, *Corydon* (Paris, 1977), pp. 8–9. The book was only made publicly available, in Gide's name, in 1924.

14 William C. Carter, *Proust in Love* (New Haven, CT, and London, 2006), p. 98.

15 André Gide, entry for 14 May 1921, in *Journal* (Paris, 1966), p. 692.

16 Edmund Gosse to C. K. Scott Moncrieff, 18 September 1921, in C. K. Scott Moncrieff, *Memories and Letters*, ed. J. M. Scott Moncrieff and L. W. Lunn (London, 1931), pp. 150–51.

17 For a brilliant account of the overlapping developments in art and science in this period, see Stephen Kern, *The Culture of Time and Space: 1880–1918* (Cambridge, MA, 1983, revd 2003).

18 Walter Benjamin, 'The Image of Proust', in *Illuminations*, trans. Harry Zohn, ed. Hannah Arendt (London, 1999), pp. 197–210 (197).

19 The issues raised by the shortened version of *Albertine disparue* caused great debate: see Nathalie Mauriac Dyer, *Proust inachevé: Le Dossier 'Albertine disparue'* (Paris, 2005); and Christine Cano, *Proust's Deadline* (Urbana, IL, and Chicago, 2006).

20 See Albaret, *Monsieur Proust,* pp. 413–15.

21 For the details of what follows, see ibid., pp. 421–33.

22 Malcolm Bowie, *Freud, Proust and Lacan: Theory as Fiction* (Cambridge, 1987), p. 52.

# Select Bibliography

## Works by Proust

*A la recherche du temps perdu*, ed. Jean-Yves Tadié et al., 4 vols (Paris, 1987–9)

*Contre Sainte-Beuve précédé de pastiches et mélanges et suivi de essais et articles*, ed. Pierre Clarac and Yves Sandre (Paris, 1971)

*Jean Santeuil précédé de 'Les Plaisirs et les jours'*, ed. Pierre Clarac and Yves Sandre (Paris, 1971)

*Écrits de jeunesse, 1887–1895*, ed. Anne Borrel (Illiers-Combray, 1991)

*Le Carnet de 1908*, ed. Philip Kolb, *Cahiers Marcel Proust*, n. s., 8 (Paris, 1976)

*Correspondance de Marcel Proust*, ed. Philip Kolb, 21 vols (Paris, 1970–93)

*Correspondance avec Gaston Gallimard*, ed. Pascal Fouché (Paris, 1989)

## Works by Proust in English Translation

*In Search of Lost Time*, trans. C. K. Scott Moncrieff (except for *Time Regained*, trans. Andreas Mayor and Terence Kilmartin), 6 vols, revd Terence Kilmartin and D. J. Enright (London, 2000–2002)

*Against Sainte-Beuve and Other Essays*, trans. John Sturrock (Harmondsworth, 1988)

*Jean Santeuil*, trans. Gerard Hopkins (New York and London, 1955)

*Pleasures and Days*, trans. Andrew Brown (London, 2004)

*Selected Letters*, ed. Philip Kolb, trans. Ralph Manheim, Terence Kilmartin and Joanna Kilmartin, 4 vols (New York, 1983–2000)

Biographical Works; Accounts By and About Proust's
Contemporaries

Albaret, Céleste, *Monsieur Proust* (Paris, 1973); trans. Barbara Bray
    (New York, 1976/2003)
Billy, Robert de, *Marcel Proust: Lettres et conversations* (Paris, 1930)
Blanche, Jacques-Emile, *Mes modèles: Barrès, Hardy, Proust, James, Gide,
    Moore* (Paris, 1928)
Bloch-Dano, Evelyne, *Mme Proust: Biographie* (Paris, 2004); trans. Alice
    Kaplan (Chicago and London, 2007)
Bonnet, Henri, *Les Amours et la sexualité de Marcel Proust* (Paris, 1985)
Carter, William C., *Marcel Proust: A Life* (New Haven, CT, and London,
    2000)
——, *Proust in Love* (New Haven, CT, and London, 2006)
——, ed., *The Memoirs of Ernest A. Forssgren, Proust's Swedish Valet*
    (New Haven, CT, and London, 2006)
Cocteau, Jean, *La Difficulté d'être* (Monaco, 1947/1983)
Daudet, Léon, *Souvenirs littéraires* (Paris, 1968)
Daudet, Lucien, *Autour de soixante lettres de Marcel Proust*, Cahiers Marcel
    Proust, 5 (Paris, 1929)
Ferré, André, *Les Années de collège de Marcel Proust* (Paris, 1959)
Gavoty, Bernard, *Reynaldo Hahn: Musicien de la Belle Epoque* (Paris, 1976)
Gide, André, *Journal* (Paris, 1966)
Gregh, Fernand, *Mon amitié avec Marcel Proust, souvenirs et lettres inédites*
    (Paris, 1958)
——, *L'Age d'or: Souvenirs d'enfance et de jeunesse* (Paris, 1947)
Hahn, Reynaldo, *Notes (Journal d'un musicien)* (Paris, 1933)
Harris, Alexandra, *Virginia Woolf* (London, 2011)
*Hommage à Marcel Proust, 1871–1922, Nouvelle Revue Française* (1923)
Maurois, André, *A la recherche de Marcel Proust* (Paris, 1949); trans. Gerard
    Hopkins, *The Quest for Proust* (London, 1950)
Morand, Paul, *Journal d'un attaché d'ambassade, 1916–1917* (Paris, 1996)
Murat, Laure, 'Proust, Marcel, 46 ans, rentier: Un individu "aux
    allures de pédéraste" fiché à la police', *Revue littéraire*, 14 (2005),
    pp. 82–93
Nordlinger, Marie, *Lettres à une amie: Recueil de quarante-et-une lettres
    inédites adressées à Marie Nordlinger, 1899–1908* (Manchester, 1942)

Painter, George, *Marcel Proust: A Biography*, 2 vols (London, 1959–65)

Panzac, Daniel, *Le Docteur Adrien Proust: Père méconnu, précurseur oublié* (Paris, 2003)

Poulet, Gaston, and Amable Massis, 'Souvenirs de Gaston Poulet et Amable Massis', *Bulletin des amis de Marcel Proust*, 11 (1961), pp. 424–8

Pouquet, Jeanne, *Le Salon de Mme Arman de Caillavet* (Paris, 1926)

Robert, Louis de, *Comment débuta Marcel Proust* (Paris, 1969)

Scott Moncrieff, C. K., *Memories and Letters*, ed. J. M. Scott Moncrieff and L. W. Lunn (London, 1931)

Sollers, Philippe, *L'œil de Proust: Les Dessins de Marcel Proust* (Paris, 1999)

Souday, Paul, *Marcel Proust* (Paris, 1927)

Steegmuller, Francis, *Cocteau: A Biography* (London, 1970)

Straus, Bernard, *The Maladies of Marcel Proust: Doctors and Disease in his Life and Work* (New York, 1980)

Tadié, Jean-Yves, ed., *Proust et ses amis* (Paris, 2010)

——, *Marcel Proust: Biographie* (Paris, 1996); trans. Euan Cameron (London, 2000)

White, Edmund, *Proust* (London, 1999)

Williams, James, *Jean Cocteau* (London, 2008)

Woolf, Virginia, 'On Being Ill' [1926/1930], in *Selected Essays*, vol. II: *The Crowded Dance of Modern Life*, ed. Rachel Bowlby (London, 1993), pp. 43–53

## Context

Bernard, Anne-Marie, ed., *Le Monde de Proust vu par Paul Nadar* (Paris, 1999); trans. Susan Wise (Cambridge, MA, and London, 2002)

Brown, Frederick, *For the Soul of France: Culture Wars in the Age of Dreyfus* (New York, 2011)

Christiansen, Rupert, *Paris Babylon: Grandeur, Decadence and Revolution, 1869–1875* (London, 1994/2003)

Clarac, Pierre, and André Ferré, eds, *Album Proust* (Paris, 1965)

Cowles, Virginia, *1913: The Defiant Swan-song* (London, 1967)

Davenport Hines, Richard, *A Night at the Majestic: Proust and the Great Modernist Dinner Party of 1922* (London, 2006)

Gamble, Cynthia, 'From *Belle Epoque* to First World War: The Social Panorama', in *The Cambridge Companion to Proust*, ed. Richard Bales (Cambridge, 2001), pp. 7–24

Garafola, Lynn, *Diaghilev's Ballets Russes* (Oxford, 1989)

Gildea, Robert, *Children of the Revolution: The French, 1799–1914* (London, 2008)

Harris, Ruth, *The Man on Devil's Island: Alfred Dreyfus and the Affair that Divided France* (London, 2010)

Kern, Stephen, *The Culture of Time and Space: 1880–1918* (Cambridge, MA, 1983, revd 2003)

Rabaté, Jean-Michel, *1913: The Cradle of Modernism* (Oxford, 2007)

Zeldin, Theodore, *A History of French Passions. France, 1848–1945*, 5 vols (Oxford, 1973–7)

Works on Proust

Assouline, Pierre, *Autodictionnaire Proust* (Paris, 2011)

Bales, Richard, ed., *The Cambridge Companion to Proust* (Cambridge, 2001)

Barthes, Roland, 'Ça prend', *Magazine littéraire*, January 1979, collected in Roland Barthes, *Œuvres complètes*, ed. Eric Marty, 3 vols (Paris, 1993–5), vol. III, pp. 993–4

——, 'Les Vies parallèles', *La Quinzaine littéraire*, 15 March 1966, in *Œuvres complètes*, vol. II, pp. 60–62

Beckett, Samuel, *Proust and Three Dialogues with Georges Duthuit* (London, 1931/1987)

Benjamin, Walter, 'The Image of Proust', in *Illuminations*, trans. Harry Zohn, ed. Hannah Arendt (London, 1970/1999), pp. 197–210

Bouillaguet, Annick, and Brian Rogers, eds, *Dictionnaire Marcel Proust* (Paris, 2004)

Bowie, Malcolm, *Freud, Proust and Lacan: Theory as Fiction* (Cambridge, 1987)

——, *Proust Among the Stars* (London, 1998)

Cano, Christine, *Proust's Deadline* (Urbana, IL, and Chicago, 2006)

——, 'Proust and the Wartime Press', in '*Le Temps retrouvé*' *Eighty Years After / 80 ans après: Critical Essays / Essais critiques*, ed. Adam Watt (Oxford and Bern, 2009), pp. 133–40

Compagnon, Antoine, *Proust entre deux siècles* (Paris, 1989); trans. Richard
    Goodkin (New York, 1992)
Finn, Michael R., *Proust, the Body and Literary Form* (Cambridge, 1999)
Fraisse, Luc, *La Correspondance de Proust: Son statut dans l'œuvre, l'histoire
    de son édition* (Paris, 1998)
——, *Proust au miroir de sa correspondance* (Paris, 1996)
——, *L'œuvre cathédrale: Proust et l'architecture médiévale* (Paris, 1990)
Hodson, Leighton, ed., *Marcel Proust: The Critical Heritage* (London, 1989)
Hughes, Edward, *Proust, Class and Nation* (Oxford, 2011)
Ladenson, Elisabeth, *Proust's Lesbianism* (Ithaca, NY, and London, 1999)
Lucey, Michael, *Never Say 'I': Sexuality and the First Person in Colette, Gide
    and Proust* (Durham, NC, 2006)
Mauriac Dyer, Nathalie, *Proust inachevé: Le Dossier 'Albertine disparue'*
    (Paris, 2005)
Tadié, Jean-Yves, *Le Lac inconnu: Entre Proust et Freud* (Paris, 2012)
——, *Proust*, Les Dossiers Belfond (Paris, 1983)
Watt, Adam, *The Cambridge Introduction to Marcel Proust* (Cambridge,
    2011)
Winton, Alison, *Proust's Additions: The Making of 'A la recherche du temps
    perdu'* (Cambridge, 1977)

## Acknowledgements

I am grateful to the School of Modern Languages, Literatures and Cultures at Royal Holloway, University of London, for the sabbatical leave and financial assistance that were instrumental in the completion of this project. I owe thanks to the staff of the Bibliothèque Nationale de France and the Réunion des Musées Nationaux; to Caroline Szylowicz and Dennis Sears at the Kolb-Proust Archive/Rare Book and Manuscript Library at the University of Illinois; and, in particular, Harry Gilonis at Reaktion, for assistance in relation to the book's illustrations. Sincere thanks also must go to Helen Buchanan and the staff of the Taylor Institute at the University of Oxford where much of the book was written. Vivian Constantinopoulos provided valuable editorial comment, support and understanding throughout the writing and production of the book, of which I am most appreciative.

## Photo Acknowledgements

The author and publishers wish to express their thanks to the following sources of illustrative material and/or permission to reproduce it.

© ADAGP Banque des Images, Paris: pp. 57, 193; © ADAGP Banque d'Images, Paris, and DACS, London, 2012: p. 162; Bibliothèque Nationale de France, Paris: pp. 107, 133, 165, 170, 180, 190; photo courtesy Bibliothèque Nationale de France, Paris: p. 95; photo Library of Congress, Washington, DC (Prints and Photographs Division): p. 50; photo © Man Ray Trust/ADAGP, Banque d'Images, Paris, and DACS, London, 2012: p. 192; Médiathèque de l'Architecture et du Patrimoine, Paris: pp. 20, 47; photos © Ministère de la Culture – Médiathèque du Patrimoine, dist. Réunion des Musées Nationaux/Félix Nadar: pp. 20, 47; Musée d'Orsay, Paris: pp. 57, 193 (conservé au Musée du Louvre, Paris); reproduced courtesy of the Rare Book & Manuscript Library, University of Illinois at Urbana-Champaign: pp. 61, 141; photo © Réunion des Musées Nationaux (Musée d'Orsay)/Gérard Blot: p. 193; photo © Réunion des Musées Nationaux (Musée d'Orsay)/Hervé Lewandowski: p. 57; photos Roger-Viollet/Rex Features: pp. 6, 17, 26, 53, 81, 84, 180, 189; The Royal Picture Gallery Mauritshuis, The Hague: p. 181; photo © Rue des Archives/Tallandier: p. 58.